Essential Flash™ 5
for Web Professionals

Lynn Kyle

Micah Brown
Series Editor

Prentice Hall PTR
Upper Saddle River, NJ 07458
www.phptr.com

Library of Congress Cataloging-in-Publication Data

Kyle, Lynn.
    Essential Flash 5 for Web professionals / Lynn Kyle.
        p.   cm. -- (The Prentice Hall essential Web professionals series)
        ISBN 0-13-091390-1
        1. Computer animation. 2. Flash (Computer file) 3. Computer graphics. 4. Web
    sites--Design. I. Title. II. Series.

    TR897.7.K95 2000
    006.6'96--dc21   00-050165

Production Supervision: Patti Guerrieri
Acquisitions Editor: Karen McLean
Marketing Manager: Kate Hargett
Manufacturing Manager: Alexis R. Heydt
Cover Design: Design Source
Interior Design Director: Gail Cocker-Bogusz
Series Design: Patti Guerrieri

© 2001 Prentice Hall PTR
Prentice-Hall, Inc.
Upper Saddle River, NJ 07458

Prentice Hall books are widely used by corporations and government agencies for
training, marketing, and resale.

The publisher offers discounts on this book when ordered in bulk quantities.
For more information, contact: Corporate Sales Department, Phone: 800-382-3419;
Fax: 201-236-7141; E-mail: corpsales@prenhall.com; or write: Prentice Hall P T R,
Corp. Sales Dept., One Lake Street, Upper Saddle River, NJ 07458.

All products or services mentioned in this book are the trademarks or service marks
of their respective companies or organizations.

Printed in the United States of America

10 9 8 7 6 5 4 3 2

ISBN 0-13-091390-1

Prentice-Hall International (UK) Limited, *London*
Prentice-Hall of Australia Pty. Limited, *Sydney*
Prentice-Hall Canada Inc., *Toronto*
Prentice-Hall Hispanoamericana, S.A., *Mexico*
Prentice-Hall of India Private Limited, *New Delhi*
Prentice-Hall of Japan, Inc., *Tokyo*
Pearson Education Asia Pte. Ltd.
Editora Prentice-Hall do Brasil, Ltda., *Rio de Janeiro*

Contents

Preface

*T*he first time I ever tried creating graphics with Flash, I loved it. By the end of the first week, I was convinced that it was one of the best Web development applications on the market. Flash 5 is a wonderful product, but if you are like me, you have no time to spend weeks learning the intricacies of every Web technology. This book is for anyone who wants a jump-start on the most commonly needed Flash techniques, and who is then interested in looking up how to accomplish specific tasks. My book is written for the Web professional desiring to learn the essentials of Flash quickly and easily.

Welcome to *Essential Flash 5 for Web Professionals*! Contained in this book are step-by-step instructions for creating wonderful Flash animations and interactive activities. This hands-on book explains how to use Flash to create

- quick-loading vector graphics
- impressive animations
- shape morphing
- buttons with actions and Web links
- buttons and movies with sound and music
- interactive movies
- simple Web forms

Several important concepts are also presented, including optimizing Flash movies for better download, detecting the plug-in, and preloading Flash.

◆ How to Use This Book

This book consists of step-by-step instructions for creating two hypothetical Web sites. The first site is a straightforward Flash site with simple vector graphics created in Flash, basic animation, animated buttons, and buttons with sound. For the second site, instructions on creating a splash screen with music and a music on/off control are given. Also covered are more advanced graphics creation and animation, an interactive dressing room, and an email form.

To use this book, follow the instructions to create the sites. As you work through the steps, you will be presented with checkpoints where you should save your work. Also, these checkpoints will give you a URL to the book's Web site, where you can download the project at that point. That way, if you ever have difficulty with some of the steps, you can get the file with these steps already completed to assist you in understanding. The Web site for this book is located at *http://www.phptr.com/essential/flash5*.

If you have any difficulty with the instructions presented in this book or if you would just like to drop me a line about it, you can reach me by email at *lynn@rainc.com*.

◆ About the Author

Lynn Kyle has been a Web professional since 1992. She has worked for the Naval Research Laboratory as a computer scientist and more recently was a Webmaster at Palm, Inc. Currently, she works for Yahoo! Inc. Lynn has received many honors for her Web designs, including *PC Magazine's* Top 100 Web Sites and *Point Com's* Top 5% of the Web, as well as print recognition in major publications such as the *New York Times, Newsweek,* and the *Los Angeles Times.* Some of the companies she has designed for include Lloyd's of London, Pfizer, and DeBeers.

◆ Acknowledgments

Many thanks to M.J. Wilson of MJ Wilson Photography *(http://www.beautybytes.com/photomj)* for the wonderful photographs and to Cheryl Boyle and Nicole Daulton for posing for them. Chrissy Rey *(http://www.flashlite.net)* provided me with very helpful advice for creating the music toggle. Thanks to Gus Mueller *(http://www.gusmueller.com)* for the sound files used in the *Stitch* site.

Thanks to Paul Saab for giving me a place to host my sites and test my work. I'm also grateful to Karen McLean and Dan Livingston for giving me this opportunity and for being so patient. Thanks to Cary Collett for the introduction and to Rachel Collett for the excellent suggestions. But most importantly, Michael, thanks for the patience. I finally finished it!

1 The Basics

IN THIS CHAPTER

- Introduction
- Drawing and Modifying Text
- Drawing and Modifying Shapes
- Texture Fills and Transparency
- Importing Graphics
- Recap
- Advanced Projects

It's 4:59 p.m. on Friday afternoon. You have just found the perfect spot to prop your feet up in your cubicle. Suddenly your boss pokes his head in. Your heart starts to pound.

"Just got out of a meeting with Mr. Big," your boss says. "He heard that all the best Web sites are now using Flash, and he wants us to as well. So what exactly is Flash?"

"It's uh...err...a really exciting new Web technology," you guess.

"Oh good, you know all about it. Here's the Flash 5 software. Mr. Big wants us to take our current home page and turn it into a Flash site by Monday. Is that going to be a problem?"

Being the ambitious, ready-to-go-home-for-the-weekend kind of person you are, you decide your best bet is to tell him what he wants to hear.

"Monday. No problem."

"I'm counting on you. Have a nice weekend!" Your boss departs, leaving you slightly lightheaded.

Okay. Don't panic. You can recreate your company's homepage in Flash and still have time to go rock climbing this weekend. Open that Flash 5 box! Let's begin with the basics.

◆ Introduction

We will start with a quick and painless overview of some of Flash's features. If you'd rather get right to creating the exciting new Shelley Biotech homepage, jump on down to "Drawing and Modifying Text."

At this point Flash should be installed on your machine. If it is not, please install it.

What's so special about Flash? Flash is an application that allows you to create quick-loading vector-based animations and full-featured interactive activities for the Web.

A vector image file consists of a list of points to be connected. Graphics used on the Web, such as JPEGs and GIFs, are known as raster graphics. Raster graphic files are much larger than vector-type files because they describe the entire image, using an x-y coordinate system. Raster graphics are much smaller because their files consist of mathematical descriptions of the graphics. Instead of each pixel of an image having to be described, a vector-based image is described in terms of connecting lines and points. In addition to being smaller files, vector images can be resized without a loss of detail.

As well as offering an efficient, streaming way to deliver vector-based animations, Flash 5 also contains a JavaScript-based programming language. The language, ActionScript, provides you with the power to perform advanced interactive tasks. ActionScript allows you to perform logical operations, string operations, and mathematical functions.

The Flash Interface

Start the Flash program. When you first begin, you will be presented with a new, blank movie, as shown in Figure 1–1.

Each movie can contain multiple scenes. A scene consists of a timeline, layers, and a work area where you create the graphics. The timeline is used for adding animation. Each scene has multiple layers, necessary for animating multiple graphics.

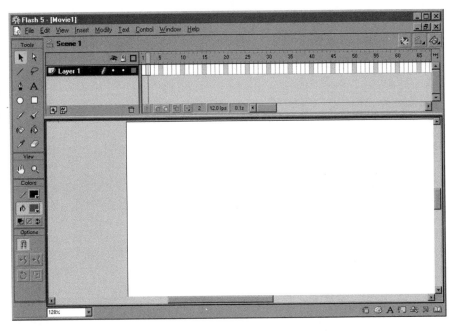

FIGURE 1–1 The Flash interface.

Drawing Toolbar

The Drawing toolbar is shown in Figure 1–2. These are the basic tools used to create and modify vector graphics in Flash. As we take a brief look at each tool, select it and notice the options underneath the toolbar change. If you hold your mouse cursor over an item on the interface for a few seconds, its name will appear.

- The Arrow tool is used to select graphic objects you have created.
- The Subselect tool defines shapes as Bezier curves and gives you handles to modify them.
- The Pen tool allows you to create shapes based on Bezier curves.
- The Lasso tool is also for selecting, but it allows you to select part of a graphic object.
- Three basic shape-drawing tools are on the toolbar, the Line, Oval, and Rectangle. If you click on each of these, you should notice that the options for the particular tool are

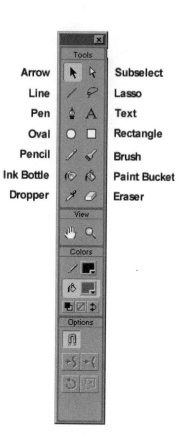

FIGURE 1–2
The Drawing toolbar.

presented at the bottom of the toolbar. This is where you can change the color, line thickness, and line style. The Oval and Rectangle also have some fill option settings.

- The Pencil allows you to draw curved lines.
- The Brush tool is for creating free-form shapes.
- If you create a shape and you want to change the line style or fill, you can edit these with the Ink Bottle and Paint Bucket.
- The Dropper is used to identify the fill color or line style in use on a particular graphic.
- The Eraser can be used to erase portions of a particular graphic.
- The Magnifier and the Hand are used to change the view of the scene as opposed to manipulating graphics. The Magnifier lets you zoom in or out, and the Hand can be used to move the entire scene around.

Movie Properties

As you create a Flash movie, you will need to modify some of the default settings for the movie, such as size and background color. These and other movie characteristics can be changed using the Movie Properties dialog box, shown in Figure 1–3. To open this dialog box, choose Modify→ Movie.

- The Frame Rate determines how many frames per second will be shown. A higher fps means your movie will play faster and be shorter, as well as seem smoother, than a low fps.
- The Dimensions are displayed in pixels. Keep in mind that Flash allows you the choice of either hardwiring the height and width or allowing the movie to scale to fit the browser window.
- The Match Printer and Contents buttons can be used to automatically set the movie dimensions based on the current movie contents or printer settings.
- This dialog also lets you change the color of the movie background
- Finally, the Units drop-box lets you change the size units used for your movie to something other than pixels.

Work Area and Zoom

The grid is a tool that helps you adjust your graphics. To demonstrate the Work Area and Zoom features, turn the grid on by choosing View→ Grid→ Show Grid. The grid should now be visible on your movie.

FIGURE 1–3 Movie Properties dialog box.

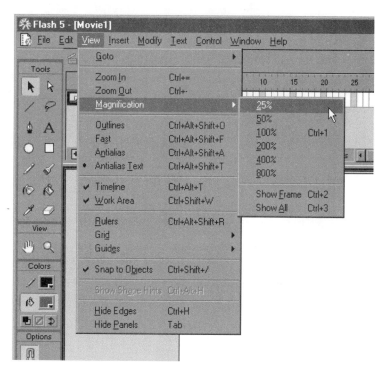

FIGURE 1–4 Magnify Menu items.

Use the Magnify tool with the plus and minus options to enlarge and shrink the movie view. You can also use the View→ Zoom In, Zoom Out, and Magnification menu options to change the view size. See Figure 1–4.

The dimensions of the movie are set in the Movie Properties dialog box. There will be times when you want to create a graphic larger than the movie height and width, or animate a graphic moving onto the movie from outside of the scene. The Work Area option under View is used for seeing graphics that are off the scene. This may be useful when you want a graphic to move on or off the scene or to be much larger than the scene itself. Figure 1–5 shows the same movie with the Work Area option turned off on the left and turned on on the right.

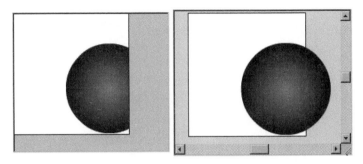

FIGURE 1–5 Work Area option shown turned off and on.

Drawing Simple Shapes and Text

Several basic shapes are shown on the toolbar: the Line, Oval, and Rectangle. The Line tool allows you to draw straight lines of varying widths, colors, and styles. Figure 1–6 shows some of the lines you can draw by selecting various attributes.

The Oval tool allows you to draw various oval shapes. They can be filled and unfilled, with or without a border. See Figure 1–7 for some examples.

To draw a rectangle, use the Rectangle tool. The options for this tool are the same as for the Oval. The Round Rectangle Radius button lets you create rectangles with curved corners. See Figure 1–8.

You can create text with the Text tool, which allows you to create text with various font styles, sizes, and colors. Figure 1–9

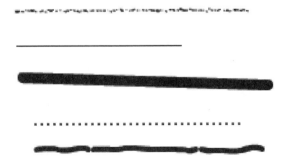

FIGURE 1–6 Line styles.

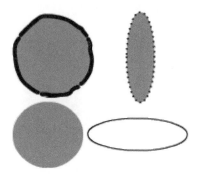

FIGURE 1–7
Assorted ovals.

shows some text with various fonts and sizes. Notice in the figure that the text is antialiased. To view the antialiased text, choose View → Antialias Text. If you choose Antialias, everything on the stage except for text will be antialiased. Changing to Antialias Text causes the text to be antialiased as well. You will probably want to do this each time you start creating a new movie. The last text example shows two different fonts in the same text string. You can change the font, color, or size at any time while you are creating text.

Undo Levels

One of the best features of Flash is the Undo Levels setting under Edit→ Preferences on the General tab. The number of Undo Levels indicated on the Edit Preferences General tab specifies how many times you can choose the Undo option. As you might guess, selecting Edit→ Undo undoes the last thing you did. Obviously,

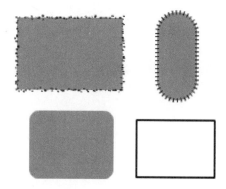

FIGURE 1–8 Assorted rectangles.

This is easy!

This is easy!

This is easy!

This is easy!

FIGURE 1–9
Assorted text fonts.

it's great if you have made a mistake, or if you just want to try out several things from the same starting point. Figure 1–10 shows the Edit Preferences dialog box with the Undo Levels set to 100. A word of caution: The multiframe nature of animations in Flash may cause you some confusion. For example, if you draw a

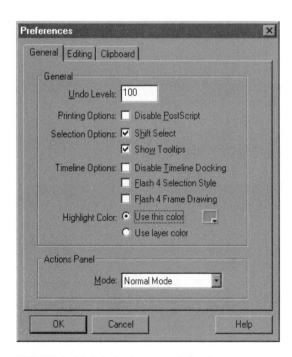

FIGURE 1–10 Edit Preferences dialog box.

FIGURE 1–11 Unselected and selected circle fills and borders.

line in one frame, change to a different frame, and choose Edit→ Undo, it will delete the line, but you won't be able to tell that it has done so unless you click on the original frame in which you drew the line.

Selecting Graphics

It is most important to know how to select and deselect graphics in Flash. To select a single graphic object, click on it with the Arrow from the toolbar. To deselect an object, hold down the Shift key and click on the object. When a graphic is selected, its appearance will change, as shown in Figure 1–11.The first circle and its outline are not selected. The second one shows just the fill selected. The third one has the outline selected, and the fourth shows both the fill and the outline selected. To select multiple objects, hold down the Shift key while clicking with the Arrow.

Enough with the preliminaries; let's start creating that page!

◆ Drawing and Modifying Text

Figure 1–12 shows the current Shelley Biotech homepage. Because the boss likes the current page, we first have to re-create it with Flash. To view the current unFlashed page on the Web, go to *http://www.phptr.com/essential/flash5/shelley/old/*. If you'd like to see where we're going, look at the finished Flash version at *http://www.phptr.com/essential/flash5/shelley/new/*. If you get tired of typing these long URLs, you should set a bookmark at *http://www.phptr.com/essential/flash5/* and navigate the site using the menus from the main page.

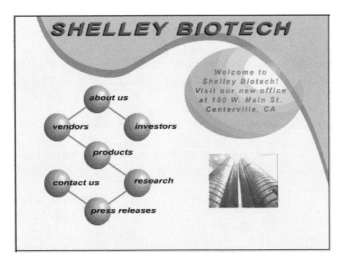

FIGURE 1–12 The Shelley Biotech homepage.

To begin creating a Flash version of this page:

1. Select the menu option File➔ New. A new blank movie opens. Next, choose File➔ Save As. Save this file in the directory of your choice as *shelley.fla*.

2. Select the menu option Modify➔ Movie. Change the dimensions of your movie to 700 pixels (px) in width and 500 px in height. You don't need to type in the px; typing in the numbers is sufficient. Select OK.

3. We will be working with the grid shortly, so let's go ahead and set it up. Choose View➔ Grid➔ Edit Grid and change the Grid Spacing in this dialog box to 20 px for both the height and width, as in Figure 1–13. Select OK.

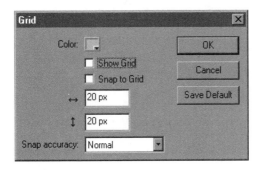

FIGURE 1–13 Edit Grid dialog box.

Since we are going to re-create the Shelley Biotech homepage, we will examine each element on the page separately. You can see that we will need to create text. Creating graphic text can be done with most graphics programs, but the advantage to creating it in Flash is that we can later animate it. Let's start by creating a layer.

Creating the Text Layer

Because we are going to work with so many different objects that we will want to animate separately, we should put each object type in a distinct layer.

1. To create a new layer, click on the Insert Layer icon below the Layer 1 label, shown in Figure 1–14. You can also use the menu option Insert→ Layer.
2. Now Layer 2 appears above Layer 1. To give Layer 2 a more meaningful name, double-click on its name so that it is highlighted and type in the words "Header Text," then press Enter.
3. Finally, click on the Header Text layer to make sure it is the currently selected one. The currently selected layer will have a pencil icon to the right of the layer name, and the layer name will appear as white text on a black background.

Setting Text Properties

We need to set the properties for our header. Flash 5 uses panels for changing just about everything. As you get more comfortable with Flash, you will want to customize your view of these panels, but for now let's stick with the default.

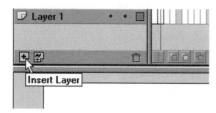

FIGURE 1–14
Insert Layer icon.

1. Choose Window→ Panel Sets → Default Layout.
2. Now select the Text Tool from the Tools menu. You will change the settings for this text in the next few steps. To make sure you are on the right track, see Figure 1–15 as you complete these steps.
3. You will need to access the Character panel to change the text properties. With the default panel layout, it should be visible in the third panel from the top. If you still don't see it, choose Window→ Panels→ Character, which toggles it on and off your workspace.
4. In the Character panel, select the Arial font from the first drop-down. If you do not have this font, substitute another one for all text mentioned in this example.
5. Select a font size of 36 from the Font Size slider control, just underneath the Font drop-down.
6. Click on the Text Color button. This is the button with a colored square on it to the right of the Font Size slider. A palette box will open. Choose the color in the fifth column and third row. We are counting columns including the first one that has primary colors and the second one that is all black. Another way to choose the color is to use the Mixer panel, located just above the Character panel. You can specify the color by RGB values, in this case 0, 102, 102, as shown in Figure 1–16. Press Enter.
7. Finally, click on both the Bold and Italic buttons on the Character panel, as in Figure 1–17.

Creating Title Text

1. Make sure the menu options View→ Grid→ Show Grid and View→ Grid→ Snap to Grid are both selected. The Snap to Grid option causes graphics to align themselves with the grid automatically.

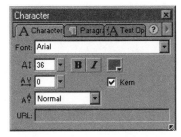

FIGURE 1–15
Character panel with Font Size slider.

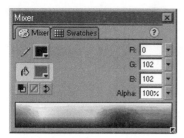

FIGURE 1–16
Mixer panel.

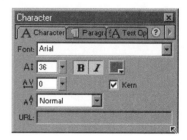

FIGURE 1–17
Character panel with correct settings.

2. With the Text tool selected, click somewhere near the upper left corner of the Scene and type "SHELLEY BIO-TECH."

3. Change to the Arrow tool. The text you created should be surrounded by a selection box, as shown in Figure 1–18.

4. Click somewhere else on the work area to deselect the text.

5. The text may look a little jagged. To view the text with antialiasing, select the menu item View → Antialias Text. The text you just created should no longer appear jagged.

6. The text needs to be stretched out. Earlier, we set the grid to 20 pixels × 20 pixels. With the Arrow tool selected, click on the Scale button, as shown in Figure 1–19. This button is located on the bottom right of the toolbar.

FIGURE 1–18 Header with selection box.

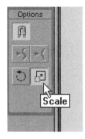

FIGURE 1–19
Scale button.

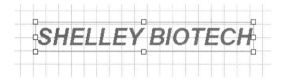

FIGURE 1–20 Selection box with handles.

7. You will now see handles on the selection box, as shown in Figure 1–20.
8. Look at the top panel on the right, labeled Info. If you do not see it, select the menu option Window → Panels → Info. This shows us the height and width and the (X,Y) locations of the currently selected object.
9. Our text is not wide enough. We want it to be approximately 600 pixels, or 30 grid lines in length. There are two ways to do this. The first way is to click and hold the right-hand center handle and drag to the right to make the text wider. The second is to change the width value to 600 in the Info panel and press Enter, as shown in Figure 1–21.

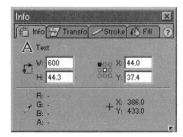

FIGURE 1–21
Info panel.

CHECKPOINT

This would be a good time to save your work. Choose File → Save As, and save this file in the directory of your choice as *shelley.fla*. Download the project at this point from
http://www.phptr.com/essential/flash5
or view it directly at
http://www.phptr.com/essential/flash5/shelley/shelley1-1.html.

Creating Shadow Text

Looking at the static Shelley page at *http://www.phptr.com/essential/flash5/shelley/old/* and at Figure 1–22, you will notice that the header text appears to have a shadow under it. Let's create this effect.

1. With the header text selected, click on the Scale button to turn off that option. The handles should disappear, but the header should have a selection box around it.
2. Select the menu option Edit → Copy.
3. Now select Edit → Paste. A new copy of the header text appears.
4. Use the Arrow to select the original header. Notice that you can select more than one object at a time by holding down the Shift key and selecting with the Arrow at the same time. If you have a selection box around both copies, click somewhere else on the screen to deselect both. You can also right-click on a PC or Ctrl-click on a Mac to bring up a menu with a Deselect All option.
5. Change the color of the current header to black by clicking on the Text Color button on the Character panel and selecting black from the palette.

FIGURE 1–22 Header with shadow.

FIGURE 1–23 Both headers selected.

6. Change to the Arrow tool. Select both header texts using the Arrow and the Shift key. Figure 1–23 shows both headers selected.

7. Select Windows → Panels → Align to open the Align panel. We are going to line up the headers on top of each other and then move the top one slightly to create our shadow effect.

8. Since the two headers are exactly the same size, you can use any of the align options. Select one of the three vertical align options, and one of the three horizontal align options. See Figure 1–24. You should now see only the green header; the black one is completely underneath it.

9. Both headers are selected, with one on top of the other. Deselect both and then click on the green header, which should be the only one visible. Using the Arrow keys to move it one pixel at a time, move it to the right 3 pixels and up 2 pixels.

10. With the Arrow, click and hold on a blank area of the scene to the left and above the headers, and drag to the right and below them. Release the mouse button. At this point, both headers are selected again.

FIGURE 1–24
Align panel.

11. Since we now have the two headers aligned appropriately, we should group them together. Choose the menu option Modify → Group. The two headers will now behave like a single object. They can be ungrouped at any time with the Modify → Ungroup command.

CHECKPOINT

This would be a good time to save your work. Choose File → Save As, and save this file in the directory of your choice as *shelley.fla*. Download the project at this point from
http://www.phptr.com/essential/flash5
or view it directly at
http://www.phptr.com/essential/flash5/shelley/shelley1-2.html.

Linking Text

We need to create the text that will be used for page links, shown in Figure 1–25.

1. A new layer for our links would be a good idea. Click on the Insert Layer button. Layer 3 now appears. Double-click on Layer 3 to rename it "Link Text." We should use Layer 1 for something, so rename it "Address Text."

FIGURE 1–25 Link text.

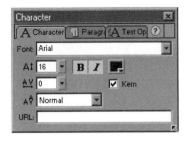

FIGURE 1–26
The Text setting for the links
and the address text.

2. Select the Link Text layer and right-click (PC) or Ctrl-click (Mac) to access the Layer menu. From the Layer menu, select Hide Others. The Header Layer will no longer be visible.

3. Select the Text tool. Use the Character panel to set the font to Arial, font size 16, font color black, and both Bold and Italic should be selected. See Figure 1–26.

4. Type the first link, "about us." Click away from the text once to finish. Then click elsewhere on the scene and type the next link, "vendors."

5. Repeat until all the links have been typed as separate objects. The links are: about us, vendors, investors, products, contact us, research, and press releases.

Now, let's add the address text to the scene.

1. Click on the Address Text layer to select it and right-click (PC) or Ctrl-click (Mac) to open the Layer menu. Select Hide Others from the Layer menu.

2. Select the Text Tool and change the text color to the green color you used for the header. The font is Arial, the size is 16, and it is both bold and italicized, just like the links.

3. Change to the Paragraph panel. The Paragraph panel is on a tab next to the Character panel you just used. If you can't find it, choose Window → Panels → Paragraph.

4. Change the text alignment by selecting the Center button next to Align on this panel, as shown in Figure 1–27.

5. Click on the scene and type "Welcome to Shelley Biotech! Visit our new office at 100 W. Main St. Centerville, CA." Use the Enter key to type new lines, as shown in Figure 1–28.

6. Select the Arrow tool. The address text should look like Figure 1–28.

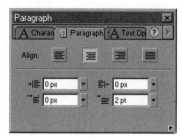

FIGURE 1–27
Paragraph panel.

7. Finally, unhide all the layers by choosing Show All from the Layer menu. It probably looks like a mess, with text overlapping. Don't worry, we'll move everything in the next section.

All the text for the page has been created!

CHECKPOINT
This would be a good time to save your work. Choose File ➔ Save As, and save this file in the directory of your choice as *shelley.fla*. Download the project at this point from
http://www.phptr.com/essential/flash5
or view it directly at
http://www.phptr.com/essential/flash5/shelley/shelley1-3.html.

Moving Text

As the last step, we will place the text objects in the appropriate locations on the page.

1. Choose the menu option View ➔ Rulers.
2. Turn off the Snap to Grid by choosing the menu option View ➔ Grid ➔ Snap to Grid. It should now be unchecked.

Welcome to
Shelley Biotech!
Visit our new office
at 100 W. Main St.
Centerville, CA

FIGURE 1–28
Address text.

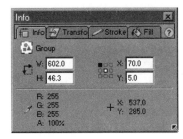

FIGURE 1-29
Info panel.

3. Click on the Header Text layer and hide the other layers using the Layer menu. The Layer menu can be opened by right-clicking (PC) or Ctrl-clicking (Mac) on the Header Text layer.

4. Make sure the Info panel is visible. If you don't see it, you can select Window → Panels → Info.

5. Change the values in the Info panel to an X location of 70 and a Y location of 5. Press Enter. See Figure 1-29. Notice using the ruler that the upper left-hand corner of the header has been moved to that location.

6. Click on the Address Text layer and hide the other layers with the Layer menu.

7. Move it to approximately X of 16 and Y of 335 on the Info panel. Press Enter.

8. Click on the Link Text layer and hide the others.

9. For now, use the Arrow to move all the link headers, one at a time, to the lower right corner of the scene. Don't worry about exact locations; we just want to get them out of the way.

CHECKPOINT
This would be a good time to save your work. Choose File→ Save As, and save this file in the directory of your choice as *shelley.fla*. Download the project at this point from
http://www.phptr.com/essential/flash5
or view it directly at
http://www.phptr.com/essential/flash5/shelley/shelley1-4.html.

◆ Drawing and Modifying Shapes

We now need to create some of the shapes for this page. We will start with the filled circles, then move on to lines, and finally to curves. You should be using a screen resolution of at least 800 pixels × 600 pixels, if possible. As we progress through this section, we will be creating many layers. You can make it easier to see the layers by clicking and dragging on the bar between the layer list and the work area, as shown in Figure 1–30. Notice how the cursor changes when it is moved over the dividing bar.

To give yourself a larger workspace, you can close any panels you don't need. Panels can be reopened at any time from the Window→ Panels menu option. Feel free to hide the rulers again by unchecking the View→ Rulers menu option. Finally, you can reduce the magnification to less than 100% using the View→ Zoom Out or Magnification options.

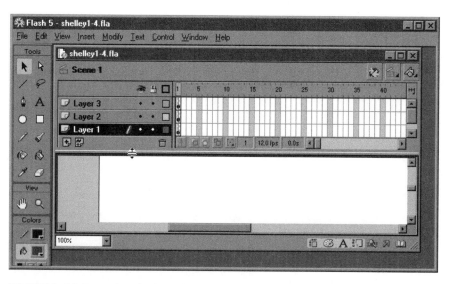

FIGURE 1–30 Dragging the layer list down to make it larger.

Creating Circles

1. Create a new layer and call it Circles. Hide the other layers.

2. If the grid is not showing, select the menu options View → Grid→ Show Grid. Make sure Snap to Grid is active by selecting View→ Grid→ Snap to Grid.

3. Select the Oval tool. You will need to set the Line Color to transparent. To do this, open the Stroke panel (Window→ Panels→ Stroke).

4. Click on the Color Palette button on the Stroke panel. Select the square with the red diagonal line across it on the upper right corner of the palette. See Figure 1–31.

5. On the same panel, select 1 for the line thickness, and Solid for the line style.

6. Open the Fill panel by clicking on the tab next to the Stroke panel. Choose a dark gray from the Fill Palette. See Figure 1–32.

7. Click and hold the mouse button in the scene to draw a circle. Make the circle 60 pixels × 60 pixels, or 3 grid lines × 3 grid lines, as in Figure 1–33. Remember that the grid is set to 20 pixels. Release the mouse button. The flat gray circle is rather boring, so we will be changing the fill shortly.

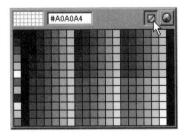

FIGURE 1–31
Setting the line color to transparent.

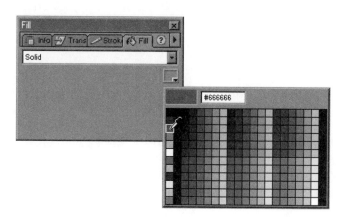

FIGURE 1–32 Fill panel.

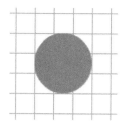

FIGURE 1–33
Circle.

CHECKPOINT

This would be a good time to save your work. Choose File→ Save As, and save this file in the directory of your choice as *shelley.fla*. Download the project at this point from
http://www.phptr.com/essential/flash5
or view it directly at
http://www.phptr.com/essential/flash5/shelley/shelley1-5.html.

Duplicating the Circle and Moving the Duplicates

You have a single gray circle, but you'll need seven of them to create the logo image seen in Figure 1–34. We will start by duplicating them. You could simply copy and paste the circles, but since we are going to change the fill later, it's much easier to make a symbol. Symbols in Flash are reusable graphics that may also have functionality attached to them. A symbol is the parent object, and each time it is used in the movie, it is an instance of the parent. Don't worry too much about definitions at this point; we will keep things simple for now.

1. Select the gray circle with the Arrow tool. The advantage to making this graphic a symbol is that it allows us to easily add more instances to the work area without having to redraw it each time. Also, only symbols can have actions associated with them, which will be important when we add code to these buttons later.

2. Choose the menu item Insert→ Convert to Symbol. In the Symbol Properties dialog box, shown in Figure 1–35, call it "Link Circle" and set its Behavior to Button. Click OK.

3. To duplicate the circle, select Window→ Library. This displays all the symbols that have been created. See Figure 1–36.

4. We have created only one symbol, the Link Circle, so far. Click and hold on the Link Circle in the Library window

FIGURE 1–34
Links with circles.

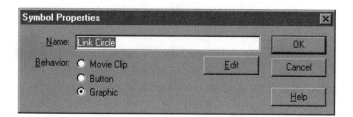

FIGURE 1–35 Symbol Properties dialog box.

and drag it to the scene. Do this a few more times until you have a total of seven circles on the scene.

5. Close the Library window and turn off Snap to Grid.
6. Open the Info panel.
7. We will now move the circles to their final locations. Move the circles to the following (X,Y) locations with the Info panel: (135, 138), (220, 80), (305, 138), (220, 196), (135, 254), (220, 312), and (305, 254). Whew!

The circles should now be in the configuration shown in Figure 1–37.

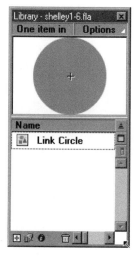

FIGURE 1–36
Circle symbol in the Library.

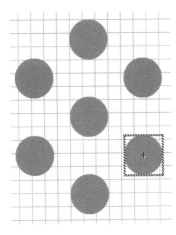

FIGURE 1–37
Circle configuration.

CHECKPOINT
This would be a good time to save your work. Choose File➔ Save As, and save this file in the directory of your choice as *shelley.fla*. Download the project at this point from
http://www.phptr.com/essential/flash5
or view it directly at
http://www.phptr.com/essential/flash5/shelley/shelley1-6.html.

Connecting Circles with Lines

As you can see from Figure 1–37, we need to draw some lines connecting the circles.

1. Select the Line tool. Use the Stroke panel to change the Line Thickness to 4, and the Line Style to Solid, as in Figure 1–38.
2. Open the Mixer panel (Window➔ Panels➔ Mixer). Click on the Pencil symbol on this panel so that you will be changing the line color, as shown in Figure 1–39.
3. Change the color to RGB of 153, 153, 102, as in Figure 1–40. Make sure the Alpha slider is set on 100%.
4. Turn on View➔ Snap to Objects. This is a different Snap than the other Snap to Grid we have used previously.

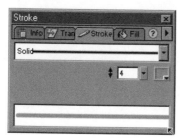

FIGURE 1–38
Stroke panel.

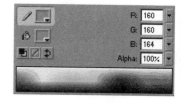

FIGURE 1–39
Mixer panel.

Snap to Objects will make it easier for us to draw connecting lines between our circles.

5. Press and hold down the mouse button at the center of the top circle. While still holding, move the mouse to the center of the circle to the right and below. Release. You should now have a line connecting two of the circles. See Figure 1–41.

6. Continue drawing lines to make an S shape, as in Figure 1–42.

7. Select all the line segments and the circles by dragging a large rectangle around everything with the Arrow tool. Choose Modify→ Group.

FIGURE 1–40
Color dialog box.

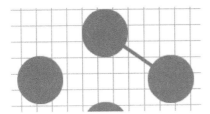

FIGURE 1–41
First connecting line.

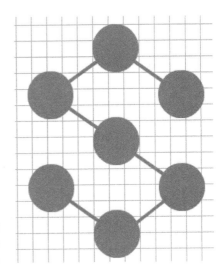

FIGURE 1–42
Circles with all the
connecting lines.

CHECKPOINT
This would be a good time to save your work. Choose File→ Save As,
and save this file in the directory of your choice as *shelley.fla*. Download the project at this point from
http://www.phptr.com/essential/flash5
or view it directly at
http://www.phptr.com/essential/flash5/shelley/shelley1-7.html.

Creating the Background Curve

The background will be created from a rectangle with one side curved. See Figure 1–12.

1. To make our animation a bit more interesting, we will make the true background color a light tan. Select the menu item Modify→ Movie. In the Movie Properties dialog box, change the Background color to the eleventh column, third row from the bottom. It's a light tan color. This color is shown as a hex value of #CCCC99 on the top part of the dialog. Click OK.

2. Time to create yet another layer. In addition to choosing Insert→ Layer, you can also create layers with the Layer menu by choosing Insert Layer from it. Name this new layer "Background." Select Hide Others from the Layer menu.

3. If all those layers are crowding the scene window, move your mouse to the border between the scene and the frame around it until the cursor changes, as shown in Figure 1–30. Click and drag upward.

4. The easiest way to draw a curve is to create a line and then modify it. Change to the Line tool. Open the Stroke panel and select black for the color, and hairline for the line style.

5. With the Snap to Grid and Show Grid options on, draw two line segments, as shown in Figure 1–43. For the first segment, click and hold and move the mouse to the right 3 grid lines and down 4 grid lines. Start the second at the end of the first and move to the right 6 grid lines and down 5 grid lines.

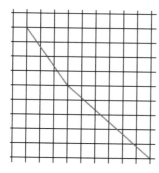

FIGURE 1–43
Two line segments.

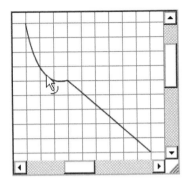

FIGURE 1–44
First line segment curved.

6. Let's turn those lines into curves. Change to the Arrow tool. Move the cursor over the first line segment. When it changes to an arrow with a curve under it, click and hold and pull the line downward until it resembles Figure 1–44. Don't forget about Edit Undo!

7. Curve the second line segment, as shown in Figure 1–45.

CHECKPOINT

This would be a good time to save your work. Choose File➔ Save As, and save this file in the directory of your choice as *shelley.fla*. Download the project at this point from
http://www.phptr.com/essential/flash5
or view it directly at
http://www.phptr.com/essential/flash5/shelley/shelley1-8.html.

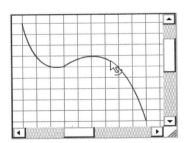

FIGURE 1–45
Second line segment curved.

Creating the Background Fill

You now have the curve that will be used to form the background. We will make it a solid filled object and then duplicate it. This is rather a long set of steps, so take a deep breath! Here we go.

1. Change to the Rectangle tool. Select black for the Stroke panel color, and hairline for the line style. See Figure 1–45.
2. The rectangle should not have a fill color. To set the fill color to transparent, click on the Fill Color button and click on the empty square on the top right of the palette. See Figure 1–46.
3. Draw a rectangle beginning with the top left of the curve and ending at the bottom right. You should now have a curve surrounded by a rectangle.
4. Change to the Arrow tool, hold down the Shift key, and click on the top and the right side of the rectangle to select both. Select the menu item Edit→ Clear or the delete key on your keyboard. You should now have a shape that looks like Figure 1–47.
5. Change to the Paint Bucket tool.
6. Open the Mixer panel and click on the Paint Bucket icon on it.
7. Set the color to RGB of 153, 153, 102, as in Figure 1–48.
8. Click inside the figure with the Paint Bucket tool to color it.
9. Delete the entire border of the shape at once by changing to the Arrow and double-clicking on the border until it is all selected. Press the Delete key and delete the outline.
10. Select the object. We are going to make a copy of this shape and offset it from the original, much like we did with the header graphic.

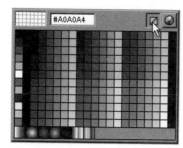

FIGURE 1–46
Setting the rectangle fill color to transparent.

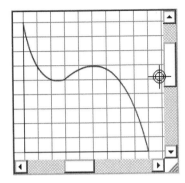

FIGURE 1–47
Second line segment curved.

11. Select Edit→ Copy and Edit→ Paste. Click and drag this copy until no part of it is on top of the original.

12. Change the color of the new object we just created. Change its color to white by selecting it, clicking the Paint Bucket tool, and setting the color to white.

13. Turn these shapes into symbols by selecting each with the Arrow and choosing Insert→ Convert to Symbol. Name the white one "White Background" and the other "Brown Background," set their behavior to Graphic, and press OK. You should have two curve shapes, as shown in Figure 1–49.

14. Select both of them and choose Window→ Panels→ Align. In the Align dialog box, shown in Figure 1–50, choose vertical align center and horizontal align center. Click OK.

15. You should now see only the white shape. If you see the brown shape, you need to change the order. Deselect both and then click on the brown shape. Choose Modify→ Arrange→ Send to Back.

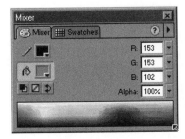

FIGURE 1–48
Mixer panel.

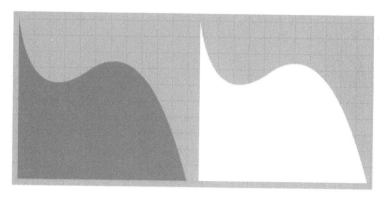

FIGURE 1–49 Two curve shapes.

16. We need to make these shapes much larger. Choose View→ Magnification→ 50%. You can tell what the current magnification is by looking at the Zoom list box on the bottom left edge of the current movie. Choose the menu option View→ Work Area and select it if it is not currently selected.

17. Change to the Arrow tool. Choose Edit→ Select All. Click and drag the shapes to the upper left corner of the screen.

18. Click on the Scale button at the bottom right of the left toolbar. Move the shapes and pull and drag the handles to make them resemble Figure 1–51. Remember, only the

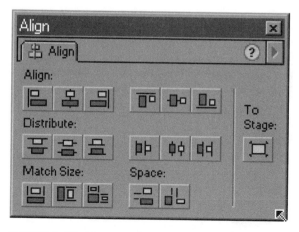

FIGURE 1–50 Align panel.

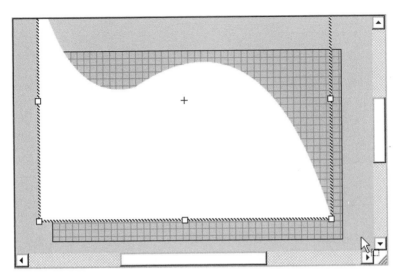

FIGURE 1–51 Moving and resizing the background shape.

white one is currently visible, but you are resizing both of them.

19. Deselect the images. Click on the top one with the Arrow and move it downward so it is offset from the brown about 40 pixels. See Figure 1–52.
20. Turn off the workspace view by unchecking View→ Work Area.

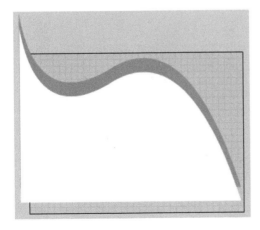

FIGURE 1–52 Alignment of background shapes.

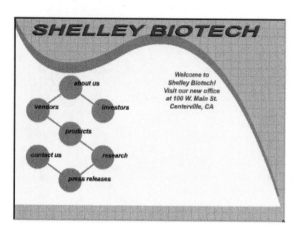

FIGURE 1–53 Current Shelley page.

21. Right-click (PC) or Ctrl-click (Mac) to pull up the Layer menu. Choose Show All from the Layer menu.
22. The background layer needs to be moved to the back. To do this, click and hold on the layer name and pull downward until you reach the bottom of the list.
23. Now that you have all the layers visible, move the graphics to roughly where they belong. You may find it easier to move the graphics if you turn off View→ Grid→ Snap to Grid. You will need to move the Link Text layer above the Circles layer. Figure 1–53 shows the current project with all the layers visible.

CHECKPOINT

This would be a good time to save your work. Choose File→ Save As, and save this file in the directory of your choice as *shelley.fla*. Download the project at this point from
http://www.phptr.com/essential/flash5
or view it directly at
http://www.phptr.com/essential/flash5/shelley/shelley1-9.html.

◆ Texture Fills and Transparency

Now that you have created the basic shapes for the page, it is time to modify some of the fills and create some textures.

Creating New Fill for Balls

Looking back at the original page, you can see that the circles under the links appear to be spheres rather than the flat gray circles we currently have. We need to create the fill.

1. Open the Mixer panel.
2. Open the Fill panel.
3. Choose Radial Gradient from the drop-down menu of the Fill panel.
4. Look at Figure 1–54. Click on the right-hand color marker, shown in the image with the cursor on it.
5. Change the RGB in the Mixer to 0, 102,102.
6. Change the left-hand color marker to white (if it isn't already) in the same way.
7. We now want to make sure we save this new gradient we created. There is a small black arrow on the top of the Fill panel. Click on this and select Add Gradient. Not only is the new gradient currently selected, it is also saved.

Changing Fill of Circles

We've created the new fill for our circles, so let's use it.

1. Click on the Symbol List button on the top right corner above the scene window. See Figure 1–55. Select the Link Circle.
2. Choose the Paint Bucket tool. The gradient fill you just created should be selected by default, but if it isn't, click on the fill on the bottom right of the palette and select it.

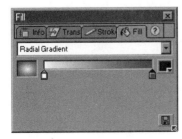

FIGURE 1–54
Fill panel with Radial Gradient selected.

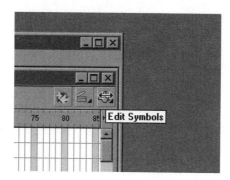

FIGURE 1–55 Symbol List button.

3. Deselect the circle. This will make it easier to see how the fill looks as it is being applied.
4. Click on the circle near its upper right corner with the Paint Bucket to apply the fill.
5. Choose Edit→ Edit Movie to return to our movie.
6. Since we made the circle a symbol, we don't need to repeat the process seven times. Changing the symbol's properties changed it for all the instances of that symbol.

CHECKPOINT
This would be a good time to save your work. Choose File→ Save As, and save this file in the directory of your choice as *shelley.fla*. Download the project at this point from
http://www.phptr.com/essential/flash5
or view it directly at
http://www.phptr.com/essential/flash5/shelley/shelley1-10.html.

Creating and Modifying the Transparent Circle

We have changed the circle fill. We now need to create a new gradient with transparency and use it for the last shape on the page. Let's start with creating the shape we need.

1. Click on the Address Text layer. If you haven't moved the address text over to the right, do so now. Figure 1–53 shows where it needs to go. Now make sure it is not

selected! This is very important. If the address text is selected, the color changes we are about to make will change its color!

2. Hide the other layers.
3. We need to create the transparent gradient fill. Change to the Paint Bucket tool. Click on the Fill Palette button on the bottom of the Tools menu.
4. Click on the gradient we created earlier. You should see it at the bottom of the palette.
5. Open the Mixer and Fill panels.
6. On the Fill panel, click on the color marker on the right.
7. On the Mixer panel, change the Alpha value to 45%.
8. Click on the marker on the left representing the white color and change its Alpha to 45%.
9. Click on the small black arrow on the top of the Fill panel and select Add Gradient.
10. Choose the Oval tool. Set the line color to transparent by clicking on the Line color palette on the bottom of the Tools menu and selecting the empty square with the diagonal red line on the upper right. The fill should be the gradient you just created. See Figure 1–56. If it is not the correct fill, click on the Palette button and choose it from the bottom of the Palette dialog.
11. Draw an oval around the text. Notice the transparency. Don't worry if it isn't perfectly placed. Just use the Arrow to move it and the Arrow with the Scale option to resize it. See Figure 1–57.
12. Click on the top layer, Link Text.
13. Create a new layer and name it "Address Sphere." Select the oval and choose Edit→ Cut. Now click on the newly created Sphere layer and choose Edit→ Paste in Place. If necessary, turn off Snap to Grid and move the oval.

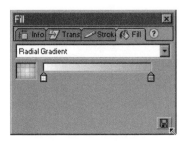

FIGURE 1–56
Gradient fill.

FIGURE 1–57
Address text.

CHECKPOINT
This would be a good time to save your work. Choose File→ Save As, and save this file in the directory of your choice as *shelley.fla*. Download the project at this point from
http://www.phptr.com/essential/flash5
or view it directly at
http://www.phptr.com/essential/flash5/shelley/shelley1-11.html.

◆ Importing Graphics

The last item you need for the homepage is the photo of the new Shelley office. You can download an image from the Web to use for importing to the page at *http://www.phptr.com/essential/flash5/shelley/misc/office.jpg*.

Importing an Image

1. Choose Show All from the Layer menu.
2. Select the top layer, Address Sphere.
3. Create a new top layer and call it "Office Photo."
4. Make sure this new layer is currently selected. Choose File→ Import.
5. Choose the image file you wish to use. The one used on the sample site may be downloaded from *http://www.phptr.com/essential/flash5/shelley/misc/office.jpg*. Click OK.
6. Use the Arrow tool to move the image to the appropriate location (see Figure 1–12). You can resize the image using the handles with the Scale option selected.

Changing the Photo Settings

If bandwidth is not an issue for your audience, you will want to control and minimize the built-in compression of imported images that Flash uses. We can change the default compression that Flash uses. In the case of Shelley's page, we want to impress our boss, so let's make the images look as sharp as possible.

1. If the Library dialog box is not opened, choose Window➔ Library to open it.
2. Locate the photo you just imported and select it.
3. Choose Properties from the Options menu. This opens the Bitmap Properties dialog box for the image.
4. Uncheck the Use Imported JPEG Data box, as shown in Figure 1–58.
5. Set the Quality to 100. Click OK.

CHECKPOINT

This would be a good time to save your work. Choose File➔ Save As, and save this file in the directory of your choice as *shelley.fla*. Download the project at this point from
http://www.phptr.com/essential/flash5
or view it directly at
http://www.phptr.com/essential/flash5/shelley/shelley1-12.html.

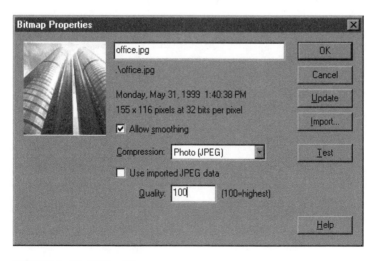

FIGURE 1–58 JPEG settings.

RECAP

In this chapter you've learned how to

- Create a new movie and modify its properties
- Draw simple shapes
- Scale, modify, and move simple shapes
- Import graphics

ADVANCED PROJECTS

1. Close the current Shelley movie and open a new movie.
2. Draw some simple lines and shapes. Try changing the options, such as color, line style, and thickness. Select them and change their color, size, and styles with the Text tool. Use the Arrow to add curves to their edges. Use the Arrow with the Scale and Rotate options to further modify them.
3. Create some text objects with different fonts, sizes, and colors. Don't forget to choose the menu option View→ Antialias Text!
4. Practice selecting and deselecting objects with the Arrow pointer.
5. Draw and modify several shapes and use the Edit Undo option repeatedly to return them to their original states.
6. Import various images of different types.
7. Use the Arrow tool with the Scale option. Notice how imported raster images, such as GIFs, JPEGs, and BMPs, look very blurry when they are scaled.

You've created all the graphics for the basic page. Chapter 2, "Animating the Page," will show you how to animate the pieces of this page.

chapter

2 Animating the Page

- Timelines and Frames
- Movement Tweening
- Shape Tweening
- Fading
- Recap
- Advanced Projects

You have totally re-created the Shelley Biotech homepage graphics with Flash. Now comes the fun part: animating it!

In this chapter you will learn the basic concepts you need to create animation in Flash movies. You will gain an understanding of what an animation is, the difference between the speed and the length of your animation, and what interface elements the Flash editor contains to help you create and control your animation.

◆ Timelines and Frames

Before we begin animating the page elements, we need to do some clean-up work, including converting some graphics to symbols and reorganizing and creating layers. You can download the current project from the Chapter 2 section of *http://www.phtr.com/essential/flash5* or directly from *http://www.phptr.com/essential/flash5/shelley/shelley1-12.html.*

Creating the Link Text Symbol

Take a look at the current page, Figure 2–1. The links on the page will all appear to move together in our animation. To allow us to do this easily, we can create a single graphic symbol that contains all of them grouped together.

1. We need to select all the text links. Use the Arrow and hold down the Shift key to select the seven text links: about us, vendors, investors, products, contact us, research, and press releases.
2. Choose Modify→Group.
3. Choose Insert→Convert to Symbol.
4. Name the new symbol "Link Text" and set its behavior to Graphic. Click OK.

Creating the Logo Layer

Flash requires that any symbol to be animated must be in its own layer. The lines connecting the circles need to be moved to their own layer, since we will be animating them. To do this:

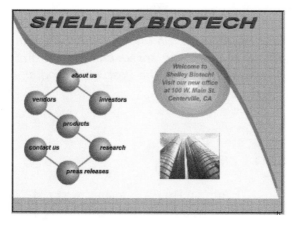

FIGURE 2–1 Current Shelley page.

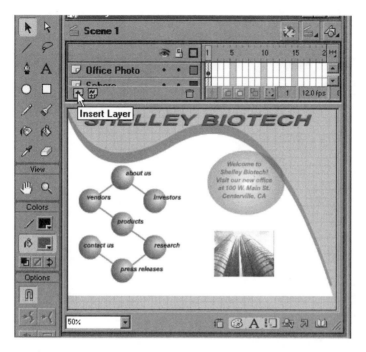

FIGURE 2–2 Flash interface with the Add Layer button.

1. Select the top layer in the layer list and click on the Insert Layer button, shown in Figure 2–2.
2. Name the new layer "Logo."
3. If you haven't already done so, move the Link Text layer over the Circles layer.
4. Click on one of the lines connecting the circles. This will select all the lines and circles, because we grouped them earlier.
5. Choose Modify→ Ungroup.
6. Choose Edit→ Deselect All.
7. Use the Arrow and the Shift key to select all of the lines. If you accidentally select something else, just click on it again with the Shift key held down to deselect it and leave everything else selected.
8. Choose Edit→ Cut.
9. Select the Logo layer.
10. Choose Edit→ Paste in Place. You have now moved the lines to the new layer. They are in front of the circles, but we'll be moving them in a moment.

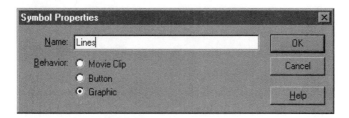

FIGURE 2–3 Symbol Properties dialog box.

11. With the lines still selected, choose Modify→ Group.
12. Finally, make the lines into a symbol by selecting Insert→ Convert to Symbol. Name this symbol "Lines" and set its behavior to Graphic. See Figure 2–3.

CHECKPOINT
This would be a good time to save your work. Choose File→ Save As, and save this file in the directory of your choice as *shelley.fla*. Download the project at this point from
http://www.phptr.com/essential/flash5
or view it directly at
http://www.phptr.com/essential/flash5/shelley/shelley2-1.html.

Adding an Additional Background Layer

Both the white and the brown curves making up the background will be animated. We need a separate layer for each.

1. Click on the Background layer. This layer currently contains both of the background curves.
2. Choose Insert Layer from the Layer menu. This will place a new layer immediately above the Background layer.
3. Rename this "Background 1."
4. Select the white curve. Choose Edit→ Cut.
5. Select the Background 1 layer and choose Edit→ Paste in Place.
6. Rename the original Background layer "Background 2."

Creating Some Layers for the Circles

The last organizational change you need to make involves moving each of the seven circles to separate layers so each can be animated separately.

1. Select the Background 1 layer and create seven new layers.
2. Name them as follows: Press Releases, Research, Contact Us, Investors, Vendors, About Us, and Products. Don't worry about the order; we will adjust that in a moment.
3. We need to move each one of our current circles to one of these new layers. For each of our seven circles, select it, choose Edit→ Cut, click on the appropriate new layer (according to the text link overlapping it), and choose Edit→ Paste in Place.
4. When all the circles have been moved, the Circles layer will have nothing left in it. Get rid of it by selecting it and choosing Delete Layer from the Layer menu.

Select and drag the layers up and down to move them. Put your layers in the following order, from top to bottom:

1. Header Text. This is the Shelley Biotech banner and associated shadow.
2. Link Text.
3. Address Text.
4. Address Sphere. This is the sphere under the Address Text.
5. Office Photo.
6. Link Circle layers. Each of the seven circles should be in a separate layer.
7. Logo. This consists of the seven lines that connect the link circles.
8. Background 1. The white curve.
9. Background 2. The brown curve.

CHECKPOINT
This would be a good time to save your work. Choose File→ Save As, and save this file in the directory of your choice as *shelley.fla*. Download the project at this point from
http://www.phptr.com/essential/flash5
or view it directly at
http://www.phptr.com/essential/flash5/shelley/shelley2-2.html.

Frames and Animation

One of the most important aspects of a Flash movie is the animation, which is nothing more than a series of still images, displayed over time. Each of these still images is called a frame. The speed at which the frames are displayed is controlled by the fps (frames per second) setting in Flash. A setting of 12 fps, which is the default setting, means that 12 frames will be displayed every second.

There are two ways to change the fps value:

1. Double-click the fps box, which is located just below the timeline. See Figure 2–4.
2. Choose the menu option Modify→ Movie.

Both of these open the Movie Properties dialog box, shown in Figure 2–5. The first blank on this dialog box contains the frame rate. A rate between 8 and 15 is recommended. This range allows relatively speedy processing of the animation while retaining smoothness of motion. For our animation, make sure the value is set at 12.

Tweening and Keyframes

Before the advent of computers, cartoon animators had to draw each frame of an animation. Although you can do that with Flash, you are provided with a time-saving method of animation that requires you to create only the most important frames. Flash creates the intermediate frames for you. This is called *tweening.* In using tweening, you create only special frames, called *keyframes,* to serve as turning points during an animation, and Flash fills in the gaps. For example, if you wanted to animate an object mov-

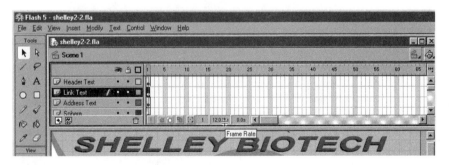

FIGURE 2–4 The frames per second box.

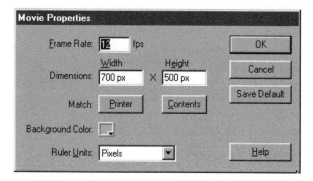

FIGURE 2–5 The Movie Properties dialog box. The frames per second rate can be changed here.

ing to the right, hitting the edge of the screen, and moving left, you would only have to create three keyframes, and tell Flash to do the rest.

Adding Keyframes to the Shelley Biotech Page

We can now put in place the keyframes we will need for the Shelley page.

1. Open the latest version of the Shelley file. This can be downloaded from *http://www.phptr.com/essential/flash5/shelley/shelley2-2.html*.
2. We now need to select the thirtieth frame of all the layers. To do this, click and hold on the frame area at the 30 frame mark of the top layer and drag downward until all the layers are selected, as shown in Figure 2–6. This is a little tricky.
3. Choose Insert→ Keyframe. Your timeline should now look like Figure 2–7.

CHECKPOINT
This would be a good time to save your work. Choose File→ Save As, and save this file in the directory of your choice as *shelley.fla*. Download the project at this point from
http://www.phptr.com/essential/flash5
or view it directly at
http://www.phptr.com/essential/flash5/shelley/shelley2-3.html

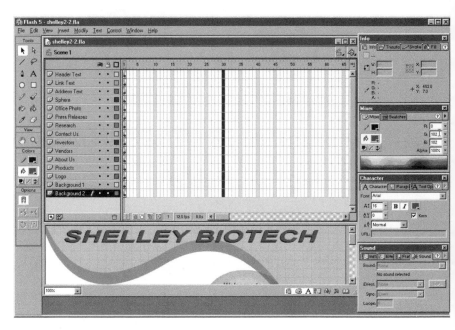

FIGURE 2–6 Selecting the thirtieth frame of all the layers.

We still have no animation, even though we have multiple frames. If you click on the first or last keyframe or any frame in between, you will notice that nothing changes. Two things still need to be done: First, you select a keyframe and make some change to the graphic at that point. Then you must tell Flash what kind of tweening to use. Flash can tween the movement of an object as well as its shape and color.

The next section will show you how to animate the graphics on this page. One final note: The graphics we created in Chapter 1, "The Basics," are the final product of the animation. We will be working backward and modifying the first keyframe, while leaving the last one alone. To get a clearer picture of this, go look at the finished product at *http://www.phptr.com/essential/flash5/shelley/new/* and notice that the page ends up looking like our current file, but looks totally different when you first see it.

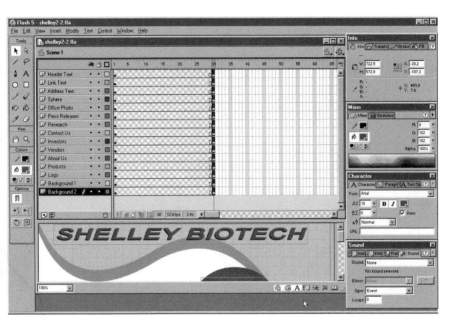

FIGURE 2–7 Current timeline.

◆ Movement Tweening

The animation you will perform more than any other will be movement tweening. This consists of giving an object a starting and an ending location and letting Flash interpolate the frames in between. Movement tweening also interpolates on the basis of object size and rotation.

Animating the Tan Background Curve

For our first animation trick, we will be making the brown background curve move. Figure 2–8 shows the path of this object. Only the outlines of the object are shown. In Flash, this view is called *onion-skinning.*

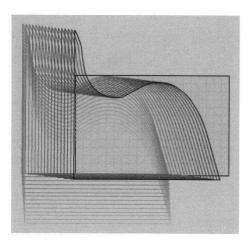

FIGURE 2–8 The animated path of the tan background object. The darker lines indicate the most recent events.

1. Begin by selecting the Background 2 layer and hiding all the others, using the Layer menu.
2. Click on the first keyframe. This is the frame located at 1 on the timeline that has a solid black circle in it.
3. You will be moving the curve partly off the movie stage. To allow you to see it, choose View→ Work Area. You may also find it useful to use the Zoom drop-down box (located on the bottom left edge of the current movie) set to 50% or smaller.
4. Change to the Arrow tool. Select the curve and move it to the left and down, as shown in Figure 2–9.
5. Add a keyframe at 14 by clicking at the 14 mark on the Background 2 layer and selecting Insert→ Keyframe.
6. Click on this new keyframe.
7. Move the curve up, as shown in Figure 2–10.
8. Click on a frame anywhere between the first and second keyframes. Choose Window→ Panels→ Frame to open the Frame panel. You can also right-click (PC) or Ctrl-click (Mac) and select Panels→ Frame from the pop-up menu.
9. Select Motion from the Tweening drop-down box on this panel. Scale should be checked, and Rotate should be set to Auto. The Easing slider should be set to 0. See Figure 2–11.

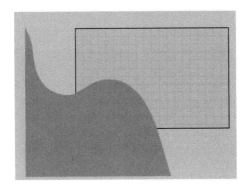

FIGURE 2-9
Tan curve location
at first keyframe.

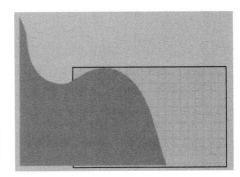

FIGURE 2-10
Tan curve location at
second keyframe.

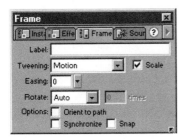

FIGURE 2-11
Frame panel.

10. Click on a frame anywhere between the second and third keyframes, and repeat step 9.
11. To test your animation, press the Enter key, or select Control→ Play.

CHECKPOINT

This would be a good time to save your work. Choose File→ Save As, and save this file in the directory of your choice as *shelley.fla*. Download the project at this point from
http://www.phptr.com/essential/flash5
or view it directly at
http://www.phptr.com/essential/flash5/shelley/shelley2-4.html

---

A Quick Word about Onion-Skinning

Flash has a very nice feature that allows you to see the stages of an animated object over time. This is known as an *onion-skin view*. It displays the graphic in each frame at the same time, giving you a picture of the path it is taking. The first frames are fainter than the later frames.

To use it, select the Onion Skin button, shown selected at the bottom of Figure 2–12. Notice the handles that appear on the timeline above all the layers. Change the frame interval by dragging the right handle to frame 30. This image also shows the Onion Skin markers on the timeline. The color changes over time, with the faintest images representing the early frames. Turn it off by clicking on the Onion Skin button again. If you only wish to see the outlines, click on the Onion Skin Outlines button.

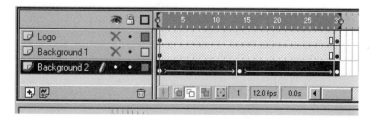

FIGURE 2–12 Onion Skin markers on the timeline.

Animating the Link Circles

The link circles will start out fairly large and centered on the Products circle. They will shrink and move outward to their appropriate places. They will also initially be transparent and fade in. Don't worry, this sounds more complex than it actually is!

1. Begin by selecting the Products layer and hiding all the others, using the Layers Menu→ Hide Others option.
2. Click on the red X next to the names of the other six link circle layers to make them appear. You should now see seven circles against the tan background, as in Figure 2–13.
3. Hold down the Ctrl key and select the fifteenth frame on each of these layers and choose Insert→ Keyframe. See Figure 2–14.
4. Select the center circle with the Arrow. The Products layer should now be selected.
5. Drag the Products layer below the other circle layers.
6. Click on the first keyframe of the Products layer, located at frame 1. The circle in this layer should be selected.
7. Open the Info panel if it is not open, by choosing Window→ Panels→ Info.

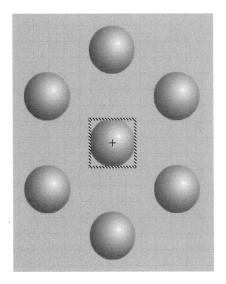

FIGURE 2–13 Link circles.

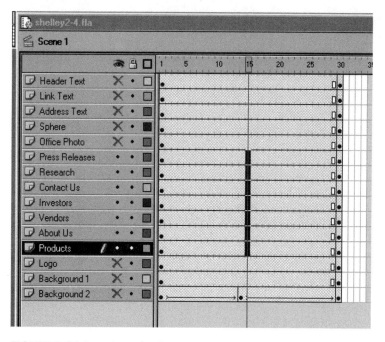

FIGURE 2–14 Inserting a keyframe.

8. On the Info panel, there is a cluster of nine small boxes. Click on the box in the center, as shown in Figure 2–15, and change the Width (w) and Height (h) each to 300. Press Enter.

9. Make sure the first keyframe is still the current one selected. Using the Arrow and Shift keys, select all of the circles.

10. Open the Align panel by choosing Window→ Panels→ Align.

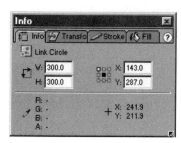

FIGURE 2–15
Info panel.

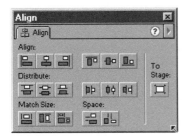

FIGURE 2-16
Align panel.

11. We want all the circles to be 300 pixels by 300 pixels and in the same location. To do this, click on the two middle buttons under the Align label. Look at the buttons shown in Figure 2–16.

12. Now click on the Match Size button on the right. This will make all the circles 300 pixels by 300 pixels and centered, so only one will be visible, with the rest stacked under it.

13. We need to set the tweening for the circle layers. For each of the seven link circle layers, click on a frame anywhere between the first and second keyframes. Open the Frame panel.

14. Select the Tweening tab on the Frame panel. Choose Motion from the drop-down list. Scale should be checked, and Rotate should be Automatic. The Easing slider should be 0.

15. Take a look at the animation you just added by pressing Enter.

We still need to make the circles start transparent and fade in. We will do this by changing the transparency for the circles at the first keyframes of each layer. This should be clearer to you in a moment.

1. Open the Effect panel. You can do this by clicking on the tab labeled "Effect" on the Frame panel dialog, or from Window→ Panels→ Effect. See Figure 2–17.

2. The Effect for the circles at the first keyframe needs to be changed. Click on the Products layer and hide the others.

3. Click on the first keyframe in this layer. The large circle visible on the stage should be selected.

4. Choose Alpha from the drop down box on this panel. Set the value to 0%.

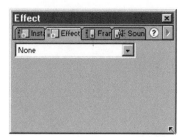

FIGURE 2–17
Effect panel.

5. Repeat steps 2 through 4 for each of the other six layers. Make sure you are making this change on the large circle located at the first keyframe!
6. Select Show All from the Layer menu.

We are getting closer, but still have a few more animations to add.

CHECKPOINT
This would be a good time to save your work. Choose File→ Save As, and save this file in the directory of your choice as *shelley.fla.* Download the project at this point from
http://www.phptr.com/essential/flash5
or view it directly at
http://www.phptr.com/essential/flash5/shelley/shelley2-5.html.

Animating the Address Text

Let's make the Address Text really large when the animation begins. It will also change color, but we'll do that a bit later in the section on Fading. To preview what the Address Text will be doing, look at Figure 2–18, which shows the onion-skinned version of the animation.

1. Click on the first keyframe of the Address Text layer.
2. Select View→ Work Area. Use the Zoom Control and change the zoom to 50% or less.
3. Use the Layer menu to hide all the layers except for the Address layer. With the Arrow, select the address text.

FIGURE 2–18
Onion-skin view of
address text animation.

Click on the red X next to the Background 2 layer to make it visible also.

4. We need to turn the address text into a symbol so we can animate it. Make sure you are on the first keyframe and choose Insert→Convert to Symbol. Name it "Address Text," change its behavior to Graphic, and click OK.

5. Now we have a small problem. The address text in the first keyframe is a symbol, but the address text in the last keyframe is not. We need to replace it with the symbol version. It's easy enough to do. Click on the last keyframe on the Address Text layer and choose Insert→Clear Keyframe.

6. Now put a keyframe back at this location by choosing Insert→Keyframe. The Address Text symbol we just created will now be present.

7. Select the first keyframe of the Address Text layer and make sure the Address Text symbol is selected.

8. Click on the Scale button on the bottom of the toolbar. Using the handles or Object Inspector, stretch the address text until it is approximately 1000 pixels wide and 1060 pixels high. You may want to do this with the Info panel instead of scaling it.

9. Reposition and resize until the word "Shelley" is located on top of the visible part of the tan curve, as in Figure 2–19. No other words should overlap the visible part of the tan curve.

FIGURE 2–19 Address text stretched and moved.

10. Click on a frame between the two keyframes on the Address Text layer. Open the Frame panel.
11. Select the Tweening tab on this dialog box. Choose Motion from the drop-down list. Scale should be checked, and Rotate should be Automatic. The Easing slider should be set to 0.
12. To see the results, press Enter.

CHECKPOINT
This would be a good time to save your work. Choose File→ Save As, and save this file in the directory of your choice as *shelley.fla.* Download the project at this point from
http://www.phptr.com/essential/flash5
or view it directly at
http://www.phptr.com/essential/flash5/shelley/shelley2-6.html.

Animating the Text Links

The text links will be very small and on the right side of the screen, then grow in size and move left. Figure 2–20 shows the onion-skinned path of these objects.

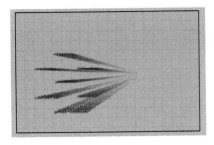

FIGURE 2–20
Onion-skin view of text links
with page border shown.

1. Begin by selecting the Link Text layer and hiding all the others, using the Layers menu.
2. Click on the first keyframe.
3. Open the Info panel and resize the group of links to approximately 40 pixels × 40 pixels and to move it to an (X, Y) location of (500, 250).
4. Click on a frame between the two keyframes on this layer. Open the Frame panel.
5. Select the Tweening tab on this dialog box. Choose Motion from the drop-down list. Scale should be checked, and Rotate should be Automatic. The Easing slider should be set to 0.
6. To see the results, press Enter.

CHECKPOINT
This would be a good time to save your work. Choose File➜ Save As, and save this file in the directory of your choice as *shelley.fla*. Download the project at this point from
http://www.phptr.com/essential/flash5
or view it directly at
http://www.phptr.com/essential/flash5/shelley/shelley2-7.html.

Animating the Header Text

Figure 2–21 shows the onion-skinned path of this object.

FIGURE 2–21 Onion-skin view of header text with page border shown.

1. Begin by selecting the Header Text layer and hiding all the others, using the Layers menu.
2. Click on the first keyframe.
3. Open the Info panel. Resize the Header Text to approximately 130 pixels by 10 pixels and to move it to an (X, Y) location of (630, 90).
4. Click on a frame between the two keyframes on this layer. Open the Frame panel.
5. Select the Tweening tab on this dialog box. Choose Motion from the drop-down list. Scale should be checked, and Rotate should be Automatic. The Easing slider should be set to 0.
6. To see the results, press Enter.

If you haven't viewed the entire page animation already, select Show All from the Layers menu. Press Enter. You have now added all the motion tweening to the page. Now let's do some Shape tweening.

CHECKPOINT
This would be a good time to save your work. Choose File→ Save As, and save this file in the directory of your choice as *shelley.fla*. Download the project at this point from
http://www.phptr.com/essential/flash5
or view it directly at
http://www.phptr.com/essential/flash5/shelley/shelley2-8.html.

◆ Shape Tweening

Shape tweening animation is used when you need to change or morph one shape into another. The shape and the color shifts gradually from the beginning graphic to the final one. As in motion tweening, Flash will interpolate the intermediate frames for you. Shape tweening is best used somewhat sparingly, as it increases the final size of the Flash movie much more than Motion tweening does.

In the Shelley Biotech page, only one object undergoes shape tweening. This is the semitransparent egg-shaped sphere underneath the address text. We will make it start out as a large S and morph into the sphere.

Creating the Beginning S Shape

Now, we need to create the starting S shape.

1. Select the Sphere layer and hide the other layers.
2. Click on the first keyframe of the Sphere layer.
3. Change to the Text Tool and open the Character panel. Set the font to Arial, the size to 72, the color black, and click on both the Bold and Italic buttons.
4. Click on the scene and type an uppercase S. Change to the Arrow Tool.
5. Select the oval shape in this keyframe and delete it with the Delete key.
6. Select the S and open the Info panel.
7. Resize the S to approximately 30 width by 155 height in pixels.
8. Choose Modify→Break Apart. This will allow us to apply a gradient fill to the S.
9. We should make the S have the same colors as the final sphere it will become. Change to the Paint Bucket. Click on the Palette button at the bottom of the Tools menu. Select the gradient fill from the bottom of the color palette that was used to fill the link circles. See Figure 2–22.

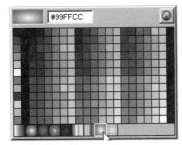

FIGURE 2–22
Gradient fill.

FIGURE 2–23
S shape.

10. Click on the S shape with the Paint Bucket somewhere near the center.

11. Click on the Header Text layer to make it visible. Make sure the S is lined up with the first letter of the header, as shown in Figure 2–23, by selecting it, moving it, and using the Scale option with the Arrow.

Now that we have our starting and ending shapes, we can perform shape tweening and let Flash fill in the frames between them.

Applying Shape Tweening to the S

1. Hide the Header Text layer and all other layers except for the Address Sphere layer.

2. Click on any frame between the starting and ending key-frames on the Address Sphere layer.

3. Open the Frame panel.

4. Choose Shape Tweening with the Blend of Distributive, and change the Easing to –100, as in Figure 2–24. Moving the Easing slider left makes the tweening start slowly and then speed up near the end.

5. Press Enter to view the shape tweening.

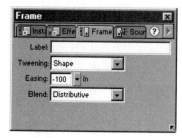

FIGURE 2–24
Tweening tab of Frame
Properties dialog box.

CHECKPOINT

This would be a good time to save your work. Choose File→ Save As, and save this file in the directory of your choice as *shelley.fla*. Download the project at this point from
http://www.phptr.com/essential/flash5
or view it directly at
http://www.phptr.com/essential/flash5/shelley/shelley2-9.html.

Adding Shape Hints

Shape hints are markers you place on the beginning and ending shapes in a shape tweening to tell Flash how to proceed in the frames between the two keyframes. When you create a shape hint, Flash puts a small, labeled circle on the image at both the first and second keyframes. You can use the Arrow to move these markers. If you place the marker at the top of the image in the first keyframe, and at the bottom of the image in the second, the image will appear to turn itself inside out, with the top migrating toward the bottom during the animation.

1. Select the first keyframe in the Address Sphere layer.
2. Choose Modify→Transform→Add Shape Hint. A small red circle with a letter *a* in it appears. Use the Arrow to move it away from the S.
3. Add two more shape hints, *b* and *c,* and move them so all three are visible.
4. Move the letters to the locations shown in Figure 2–25.
5. Click on the last keyframe. Matching letters are stacked in the center of the oval. Move them to the locations shown

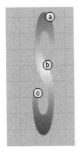

FIGURE 2–25
Shape hints correctly
placed on the S graphic.

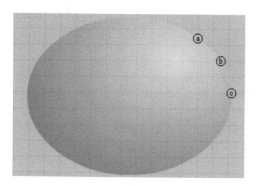

FIGURE 2-26 Shape hints correctly placed on
the transparent oval.

in Figure 2-26. These will turn green when they are in
valid locations.

6. Press Enter to see the result of the shape hint influence on
the shape tweening.
7. To hide the shape hints from the view, uncheck
View→ Show Shape Hints.

CHECKPOINT

This would be a good time to save your work. Choose File→ Save As,
and save this file in the directory of your choice as *shelley.fla*. Download the project at this point from
http://www.phptr.com/essential/flash5
or view it directly at
http://www.phptr.com/essential/flash5/shelley/shelley2-10.html.

If you make all the layers visible at this point and animate
them, you'll notice that the page is rather cluttered. We will fix
that in the next section.

◆ Fading

Now all that remains to be done is to apply some fading to the
beginning keyframes of some of the images. This will help to

clean up much of the clutter you see when you view the entire animation.

Fading in the White Background

The white background layer is nice for the final frame of the animation, but is a bit distracting while the animation is taking place. Let's make it fade in.

1. We made the white background a symbol in Chapter 1. This allows us to modify its Instance Properties. Select the Background 1 layer and hide all the rest.
2. Click on the first keyframe.
3. With the Arrow, select the white curve. Open the Effect panel.
4. Choose Alpha from the drop-down list and set the value to 0% by moving the slider down or typing in the text box. See Figure 2–27. Press Enter.
5. Click on a frame between the two keyframes on the White Background layer. Open the Frame panel.
6. Choose Motion from the drop-down list. Scale should be checked, and Rotate should be Automatic. Easing should be set to 0. Press Enter.
7. To see the results, press Enter.

CHECKPOINT
This would be a good time to save your work. Choose File→ Save As, and save this file in the directory of your choice as *shelley.fla.* Download the project at this point from
http://www.phptr.com/essential/flash5
or view it directly at
http://www.phptr.com/essential/flash5/shelley/shelley2-11.html.

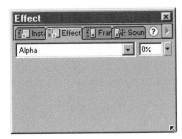

FIGURE 2–27
Effect panel.

Fading in the Office Photo

The office photo will also fade in. The procedure is basically the same as before, except that the fade-in will begin at the fifteenth frame.

1. Select the Office Photo layer and hide all the rest.
2. Click on the first keyframe.
3. With the Arrow, select the photo.
4. We need to make the photo a symbol so we can modify its transparency. Choose Insert→ Convert to Symbol. Name it "Photo," set its behavior to Graphic, and click OK.
5. Click on the keyframe at 30 and choose Insert→ Clear Keyframe. This will remove the keyframe at 30 that does not have the Photo symbol in it. The photo in this frame was not the photo symbol you created in step 4. To create the fade effect, it must be the same symbol.
6. Now add a keyframe to 30 again by choosing Insert→ Keyframe. This time the photo image will be the Photo symbol you created.
7. Click on the first keyframe again. Select the photo.
8. Open the Effect panel.
9. Choose Alpha from the drop-down list and set the value to 0% by moving the slider down or typing in the text box. See Figure 2–27. Press Enter.
10. Click on the fifteenth frame and choose Insert→ Keyframe.
11. Click on a frame between the second and third keyframes on the Office Photo layer. Open the Frame panel.
12. Choose Motion from the drop-down list. Scale should be checked, and Rotate should be Automatic. Easing should be set to 0. Press Enter.
13. Press Enter to see the result. The fade-in begins at the fifteenth frame and finishes at the thirtieth.

CHECKPOINT

This would be a good time to save your work. Choose File→ Save As, and save this file in the directory of your choice as *shelley.fla*. Download the project at this point from
http://www.phptr.com/essential/flash5
or view it directly at
http://www.phptr.com/essential/flash5/shelley/shelley2-12.html.

Fading in the Logo Lines

The lines connecting the link circles should also be faded in.

1. Select the Logo layer and hide all the rest.
2. Click on the first keyframe.
3. With the Arrow, select the lines. Open the Effect panel.
4. Choose Alpha from the drop-down list and set the value to 0% by moving the slider down or typing in the text box. See Figure 2–27. Press Enter.
5. Click on a frame between the two keyframes. Open the Frame panel.
6. Choose Motion from the drop-down list. Scale should be checked, and Rotate should be Automatic. Easing should be set to 0. Press Enter.
7. Press Enter to see the result.

CHECKPOINT
This would be a good time to save your work. Choose File➔ Save As, and save this file in the directory of your choice as *shelley.fla*. Download the project at this point from
http://www.phptr.com/essential/flash5
or view it directly at
http://www.phptr.com/essential/flash5/shelley/shelley2-13.html.

Changing the Color of the Text Links

Instead of fading in the text links, we will make the color change. The color will start out the same as the background and then will change to black. This will make the links stand out a bit more than if they were faded in.

1. Select the Link Text layer and hide all the rest.
2. Click on the first keyframe.
3. With the Arrow, select the links. Open the Effect panel.
4. Choose Tint from the drop-down list.
5. Set the Tint Amount percentage to 100.
6. Change the color values on this panel to a red of 204, green of 204, and blue of 153, as shown in Figure 2–28. Press Enter.

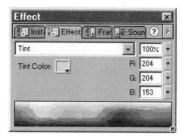

FIGURE 2–28
The Effect panel with the
RGB set appropriately.

7. We don't need to add motion tweening for this layer since we did that earlier when we made the Link Text start small and get larger. To see the results, press Enter.

CHECKPOINT

This would be a good time to save your work. Choose File→ Save As, and save this file in the directory of your choice as *shelley.fla*. Download the project at this point from
http://www.phptr.com/essential/flash5
or view it directly at
http://www.phptr.com/essential/flash5/shelley/shelley2-14.html.

Changing the Color of the Address Text

Right now, the Address Text symbol starts out very large and dominates the screen. If we change the color of it to the background of our movie, only the word "Shelley" that is over the brown background curve will be visible. We can then make its color change to black as it gets smaller.

1. Select the Address Text layer and hide the others.
2. Click on the first keyframe.
3. The Address Text symbol should now be selected. Open the Effect panel.
4. Choose Tint from the drop-down list and set the Tint Amount percentage to 100.
5. Change the color values to a red of 204, green of 204, and blue of 153, as shown in Figure 2–28. Click OK.
6. Again, we added the Motion tweening earlier, so we do not need to do that now. To see the results, press Enter.

CHECKPOINT

This would be a good time to save your work. Choose File→ Save As, and save this file in the directory of your choice as *shelley.fla*. Download the project at this point from
http://www.phptr.com/essential/flash5
or view it directly at
http://www.phptr.com/essential/flash5/shelley/shelley2-15.html.

You have created the graphics for the homepage and animated them. In the next chapter, "Making the Page Interactive," you will add buttons and links to make the page interactive, and we will examine symbols and buttons in depth.

RECAP

In this chapter you've learned how to
- Create symbols and animate them
- Animate the color of symbols
- Animate symbols fading
- Morph shapes

ADVANCED PROJECTS

1. In a new movie, create several layers with a graphic in each and turn these into symbols.
2. Create a layer with a different graphic at different keyframes.
3. Use shape tweening to morph one shape into another.
4. Try adding shape hints to control the morphing.
5. Animate them so they appear to collide.
6. Use fading and color effects on them before and after the collision.

3 Making the Page Interactive

IN THIS CHAPTER

- Symbols
- Creating Buttons
- Button Actions
- Sound Effects
- Recap
- Advanced Projects

The Shelley Biotech page has been created and animated, but it still lacks an important element that Flash offers: interactivity. We will start with a brief overview of symbols, important devices for creating interactivity. Then you will learn how to create buttons that will respond to mouse cursor actions. Finally, you'll learn how to add sound to your Flash movie.

◆ Symbols

Flash symbols are graphic objects that are stored by Flash. One of the features of symbols that make them so important is their reusability. When you create a symbol, you can use it over and over again without having to redraw it each time you need it.

And if you decide to change it, you don't need to change each copy, or instance, of it; you can simply change the stored master symbol. Changing the master symbol changes all the instances of it in your Flash movie.

There are three types of symbols: graphics, buttons, and movie clips. Graphics are noninteractive images to which animation and sounds can be attached. Buttons are graphics that can also respond to mouse actions. Movie clips are entire Flash movies that can be duplicated dynamically, dragged, and reused inside other movies.

There are few basic tasks you should know: how to create a symbol, how to interact with a symbol library, how to edit a symbol, and how to change its type.

Creating Symbols

In the earlier chapters, we created many symbols. There are two ways to create a symbol. After you have created a graphic you want to convert, you can either choose the menu option Insert→ Convert to Symbol or press the F8 key. Once you have created the symbol, it is automatically stored in the local library.

Using the Library to Access Your Symbols

To see all the symbols you have in your movie, open the Library, using the menu option Window→ Library or Ctrl-L (PC) or Command-L (Mac). You can see the Library window in Figure 3–1. The Library stores not only the symbols used in your movie, but also any other importable media you have used, such as sound files and bitmaps.

Each movie has a library associated with it, and Macromedia also ships with some media libraries, which are collections of sounds, buttons, movies, and prebuilt form elements for you to use in your own Flash applications. Unlike movie libraries, these libraries cannot be modified. To use items from these libraries, you must drag them onto your movie. They will then appear in your local library. You can access the Macromedia libraries under the menu item Window→ Common Libraries.

Editing Symbols

There are several ways to edit symbols. In the Library, you can select the symbol you wish to edit and pull up the Symbol menu

FIGURE 3–1
Library dialog box.

by clicking on the Options button on the top right and selecting Edit. The Symbol menu allows you to create, delete, modify, copy, and file symbols in subfolders for better organization. You can also choose Edit→ Edit Symbols. Symbol editing mode allows you to change the appearance, animation, and actions associated with a symbol without having to change the movie in which the symbol appears. When you switch to symbol editing mode, the name of the symbol appears underneath the filename at the top of the movie. Figure 3–2 shows the symbol editing mode for the Brown Background symbol. Once you are in symbol editing mode, you can switch between symbols by using the Symbol List button on the top right side of the window.

Changing Symbol Types

In this chapter, we will be modifying the buttons we created earlier to add functionality and sound. Before we do that, however, we will also change one of our graphic symbols we created earlier into a button. You can change any symbol's type from one type to another with the Symbol Properties dialog box. Selecting the symbol in the Library and choosing Properties from the Options menu on the Library dialog box will access this dialog box. You can then change the type by clicking on the appropriate radio button, as seen in Figure 3–3.

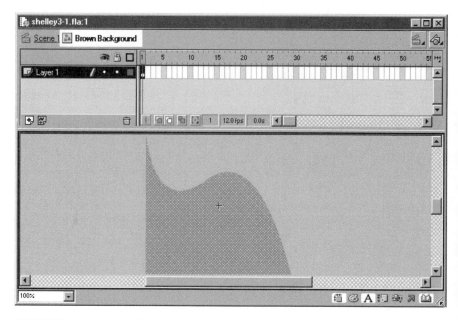

FIGURE 3-2 Symbol editing mode for Brown Background symbol.

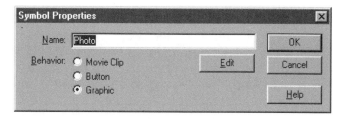

FIGURE 3-3 Symbol Properties dialog box.

◆ Creating Buttons

Unlike symbols, buttons allow you to attach actions to them. This means that buttons can change colors, make sounds, and serve as links to new pages when they are pressed. All buttons have four special frames that can be assigned actions: Up, Over, Down, and Hit. These refer to mouse cursor locations. Up is the default state of the button when the cursor is not touching it. Over means the cursor is overlapping the button. Down is the same as Over, except that the mouse button is pressed. Hit is used to define an area around the button. We will learn how to add these properties in the next section.

Here is a possible scenario for why you would need to change your symbol type: Your boss, on his way to the golf course Saturday morning, stops by to see how you are doing. As you frantically hide your game of Freecell from him, you pop up the latest version of the Shelley homepage to impress him. He's quite impressed with the animation you have added, but throws a wrench into the works by suggesting that you do "something interesting" with the office photo. Thinking quickly, you suggest that when the site visitor's mouse goes over it, office directions should appear to the right of it. Your boss is completely impressed, and heads off to spend a fun day hitting a small ball with a stick.

Changing the Photo Symbol's Properties

The Photo is now a graphic symbol. Let's start by changing it to a button.

1. Open the Library dialog box by selecting Window→ Library.
2. In the scroll-down list, select the Photo symbol. Choose Properties from the Options menu, as shown in Figure 3–4.
3. Change the behavior to Button and click OK.

Changing the Instance Properties for the Photo

1. Right-click (PC) or Ctrl-click (Mac) on the Office Photo layer. Choose Hide Others from the Layers menu.
2. Click on the last keyframe of the Office Photo layer.

FIGURE 3–4 Symbol Properties dialog box.

FIGURE 3–5
Instance panel.

3. Click on the office photo, visible on the stage.
4. Open the Instance panel.
5. On the Behavior drop-down, change the behavior to Button. See Figure 3–5.

CHECKPOINT
This would be a good time to save your work. Choose File→ Save As, and save this file in the directory of your choice as *shelley.fla.* Download the project at this point from
http://www.phptr.com/essential/flash5
or view it directly at
http://www.phptr.com/essential/flash5/shelley/shelley3-1.html.

By changing the office photo to be a button in the last keyframe, and leaving the first and middle keyframes as graphics, we are telling Flash to treat it as a button after the thirtieth keyframe and from then on. The point of this will become more obvious after we apply some button frame actions.

Adding the Mouse-Over Action for the Office Photo

Making directions appear when the mouse goes over the office photo is quite simple; we will simply change its Over frame to contain the direction text.

1. Right-click (PC) or Ctrl-click (Mac) on the Office Photo layer and choose Show All from the Layers menu.
2. Click on the last keyframe of the Office Photo layer.

3. Right-click (PC) or Ctrl-click (Mac) on the office photo in this keyframe.
4. Choose Edit in Place. The other graphics on the page are grayed out but still visible.
5. Click on the Over frame in the timeline, shown in Figure 3–6. Choose Insert→ Keyframe.

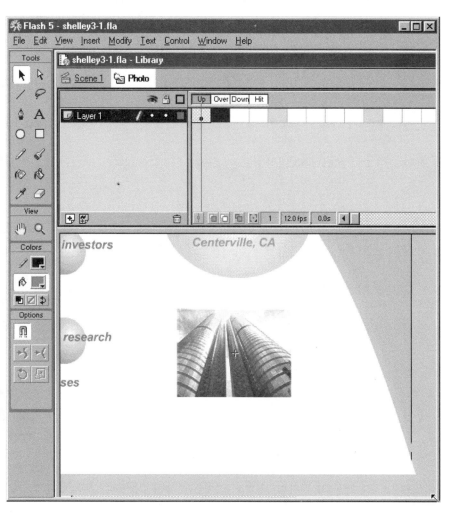

FIGURE 3–6 Over keyframe of Office Photo button.

6. Pick an area on the tan background above and to the right that looks like a good place for us to put our office directions. Change to the Text tool and type in some directions to get to Shelly's office. You will probably want to choose Arial 12-point black font to match the other text on the page. Make sure you are doing this with the Over keyframe selected!
7. Choose Edit→ Edit Movie to return to Movie editing mode.
8. To see the result, choose Control→ Enable Simple Buttons. When your mouse goes over the office photo, the directions appear! Remember to turn off Enable Simple Buttons when you are done.

Adding the Web Links to the Buttons

Now we can make the circles link to the appropriate subpages when they are clicked on.

1. Click on the last keyframe.
2. Right-click (PC) or Ctrl-click (Mac) on the "about us" link circle.
3. Choose Actions.
4. Click on Basic Actions in the left part of the Object Actions dialog. Double-click on Get URL from the menu.
5. Type the URL of your choice or use the hypothetical Shelley address, *http://www.phptr.com/essential/flash5/shelley/about.html,* in the URL box on the bottom of the dialog. See Figure 3–7.
6. Leave this dialog open and click on one of the other link circles. The actions on the right will disappear, but don't worry! This dialog remembers the actions associated with each object. To confirm this, feel free to click on the "about us" circle again and you will see that the code is still there.
7. Repeat this process of adding URLs for each of the link circles, linking to the pages *vendors.html, investors.html, products.html, contact.html, research.html,* and *press.html,* as appropriate. Close the dialog by clicking on the X on the upper right of the dialog when you are finished.

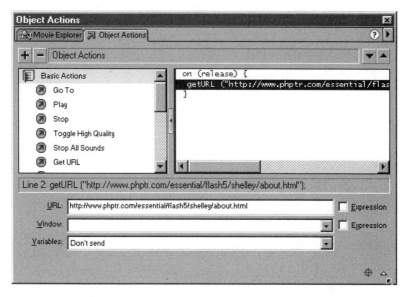

FIGURE 3-7 Adding the URL to the action.

CHECKPOINT
This would be a good time to save your work. Choose File➔ Save As, and save this file in the directory of your choice as *shelley.fla*. Download the project at this point from
http://www.phptr.com/essential/flash5
or view it directly at
http://www.phptr.com/essential/flash5/shelley/shelley3-2.html.

Testing the Links

At this point, there is no easy way to test the URLs you have just added. You can tell whether or not a URL link exists, but you can't tell what the link is without actually publishing the movie or checking the Instance Properties for the buttons. Let's take a peek at how the buttons will behave. Choose Control➔ Enable

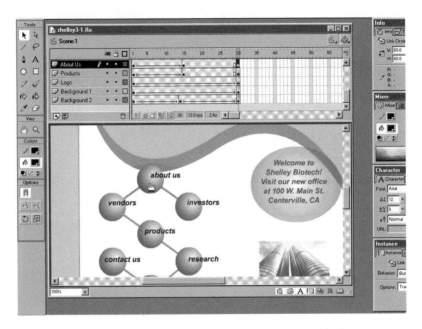

FIGURE 3–8 The cursor changes to a link-hand cursor over the button.

Simple Buttons. As you move your mouse over the buttons in frames 15 to 30, the mouse cursor will change to a link-hand cursor, as shown in Figure 3–8. When you are done, uncheck the Control→Enable Simple Buttons option.

◆ Button Actions

Four actions are associated with each button. When we created the Link Circle symbol, we set its symbol type to Button.

Opening the Button Frame Action Window

When you created the Link Circle button, the four frame actions were added to it. To access them:

1. Open the Window→Library dialog box.
2. Scroll down and select the Link Circle symbol.
3. Click on the Options menu, as shown in Figure 3–9, and choose Edit. The four frames for our button are now visible.

FIGURE 3–9
Choosing Edit from
the Options menu.

4. Double-click on the Layer 1 label and change its name to "Action." Fortunately, we will have to set the action only once for the Link Circle symbol instead of setting it multiple times, once for each link circle.

Adding the Keyframes for Button Actions

The three actions we need to edit do not have keyframes. Let's add them.

1. Click directly beneath the word "Over" in the Action layer timeline.
2. Choose Insert→ Keyframe. A small dot should appear, as shown in Figure 3–10.
3. Click directly beneath the word "Down" in the Action layer timeline.
4. Choose Insert→ Keyframe.

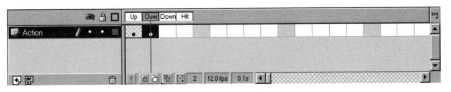

FIGURE 3–10 Keyframe inserted at the Over frame.

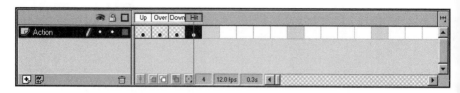

FIGURE 3–11 All of the button keyframes inserted.

5. Click directly beneath the word "Hit" in the Action layer timeline.
6. Choose Insert→ Keyframe. Your Action layer should now look like Figure 3–11.

To edit each frame, you will click on the keyframe below it. Each frame starts out looking like the beginning one. Let's work on the Hit frame first.

Creating the Hit Frame

The Hit frame defines the area around the button that will serve as the link to the URLs we added earlier. On the Shelley page, both the button and the text link to the right of it should be clickable.

1. You should be in symbol editing mode for the Link Circle symbol. The symbol name "Link Circle" should appear above the timeline.
2. Click on the Hit keyframe. Click on the stage to deselect the link circle.
3. Use the Rectangle tool, the Line and Fill color both set to black, a Line Thickness of 1.0, and a Solid Line Style. See Figure 3–12.
4. Draw a rectangle to the right of the link circle, as shown in Figure 3–13.

CHECKPOINT
This would be a good time to save your work. Choose File→ Save As, and save this file in the directory of your choice as *shelley.fla*. Download the project at this point from
http://www.phptr.com/essential/flash5
or view it directly at
http://www.phptr.com/essential/flash5/shelley/shelley3-3.html.

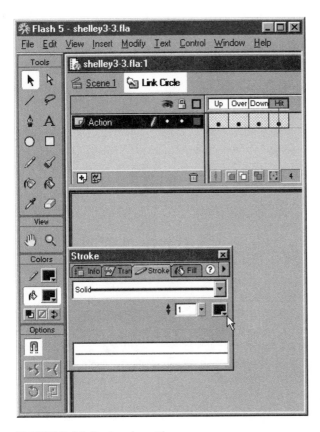

FIGURE 3–12 Rectangle settings.

FIGURE 3–13
Rectangle defining the hit area.

Creating the Over Frame

We will change the appearance of the button when the mouse cursor runs over it.

1. You should be in symbol editing mode for the Link Circle symbol. Click on the Over frame. Your workspace should look like Figure 3–14.
2. Click somewhere on the stage to deselect the circle. We will now create a new texture to fill this circle.
3. Click on the Fill panel. Choose Radial Gradient from the drop-down list.
4. The fill we used on the circles is now visible.
5. Look at Figure 3–15. Click on the right-hand color marker.
6. Open the Mixer panel. Change the RGB in this panel to 153, 153, 102.

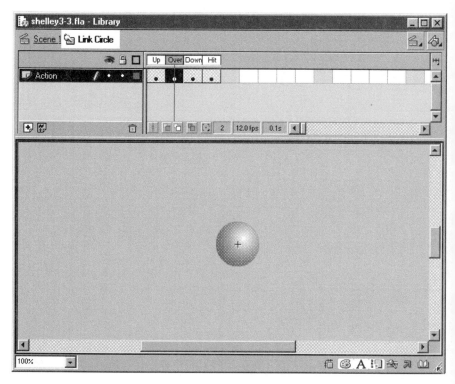

FIGURE 3–14 Workspace with the Over frame selected.

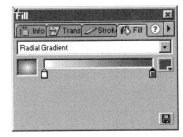

FIGURE 3–15
Fill panel.

7. There is a small black arrow on the top right of the Fill panel. Click on this and choose Add Gradient.

8. Click on the circle on the stage with the arrow. It is now selected.

9. Change to the Paint Bucket tool. Click on the Fill Color palette button on the toolbar. Select the tan and white gradient fill we just created.

10. To check the change you just made, click on each of the keyframes. Notice that the Over frame is different from the other three.

CHECKPOINT
This would be a good time to save your work. Choose File→ Save As, and save this file in the directory of your choice as *shelley.fla*. Download the project at this point from
http://www.phptr.com/essential/flash5
or view it directly at
http://www.phptr.com/essential/flash5/shelley/shelley3-4.html.

Creating the Down Frame

This will change the appearance of the button when it is clicked on.

1. You should be in symbol editing mode for the Link Circle symbol. Click on the Down frame.

2. Click somewhere on the stage to deselect the circle. We will now create a new texture to fill this circle.

3. Open the Fill panel.

4. The fill we used on the circles is now visible.

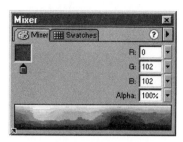

FIGURE 3–16
Mixer panel.

5. Click on the right-hand color marker.
6. Open the Mixer panel. Change the RGB to 255, 255, 255. Click on the left-hand color marker. Change the RGB to 0, 102, 102, shown in Figure 3–16.
7. There is a small black arrow on the top right of the Fill panel. Click on this and choose Add Gradient.
8. Click on the circle on the stage with the arrow. It is now selected.
9. Change to the Paint Bucket tool. Click on the Fill Color palette button on the toolbar. Select the gradient fill we just created.
10. To check the change you just made, click on each of the keyframes. Notice that the Down frame is different from the other three, shown in Figure 3–17.

CHECKPOINT
This would be a good time to save your work. Choose File→ Save As, and save this file in the directory of your choice as shelley.fla. Download the project at this point from
http://www.phptr.com/essential/flash5
or view it directly at
http://www.phptr.com/essential/flash5/shelley/shelley3-5.html.

Testing the Button Actions

The area of the button that will act as a link and respond to mouse actions is now defined. You can test the changes you just made.

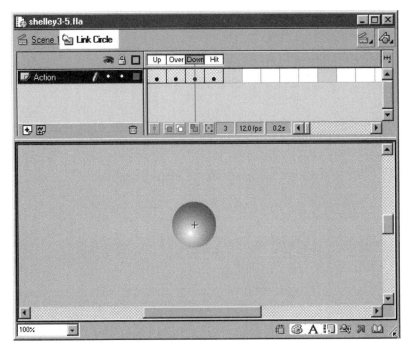

FIGURE 3–17 Button appearance at the Down keyframe.

1. Choose the menu option Edit→ Edit Movie.
2. You are now presented with your current scene. Select Control→ Enable Simple Buttons.
3. Click on the last frame of your animation.
4. Move your mouse over the buttons and click on them to see the actions.
5. When you are through, uncheck the Control→ Enable Simple Buttons option.

◆ Sound Effects

Our buttons now respond to mouse motions and clicks. We can also add a sound to them that will play when they are clicked. Macromedia ships a library of sounds for your use. We will be using one of them, but first you will see how to add your own *.wav* file if you desire.

Adding a Sound to the Library

First we need to add the button sound to the current Library. This will then allow us to add it to the button.

1. Open the Library window by choosing Window→ Library.
2. Choose File→ Import.
3. Select a sound file from your disk, such as a WAV (PC) or an AIFF (Mac).
4. The file now appears in your Library window.

Using the Macromedia Sounds Library

Using a sound from the Macromedia Sounds Library is a bit trickier.

1. Open the Macromedia Sounds Library by choosing the menu option Window→ Common Libraries→ Sounds.
2. The window shown in Figure 3–18 will open.
3. Preview the various sounds by clicking on the Play button, the arrow pointing to the right.

We have to create a layer for the sound before we can add it to our button.

FIGURE 3–18
Macromedia Sounds Library dialog box.

Adding Sound to the Buttons

Adding sound to the buttons is done in symbol editing mode.

1. Scroll through the list on the Library dialog box and click on the Link Circle symbol. Click on the Options button on the upper right of the dialog box and choose Edit. You are now in symbol editing mode.
2. You should see the frames we added earlier for the button actions. We need to add a new layer for the sound. Choose Insert→Layer.
3. Rename the new layer "Sounds" by double-clicking on its name and typing it in. See Figure 3–19.
4. Click under the Down frame on the Sounds layer and choose Insert→Keyframe. See Figure 3–20.
5. Drag the sound you wish to use from the Library to the Link Circle symbol editing window. If you want to use the Macromedia sound, you will drag from the Sounds Library. If you want to use a sound you added to the local Library, select and drag that one.
6. Click the Down keyframe of the Sounds layer.
7. To see and change the properties of this sound, open the Sound panel, as shown in Figure 3–21.

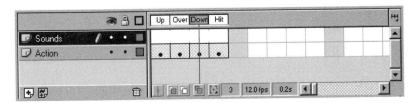

FIGURE 3–19 Sounds layer added to the link circle.

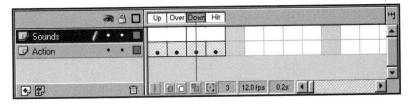

FIGURE 3–20 Keyframe added to the Down frame of the Sounds layer.

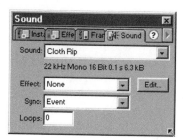

FIGURE 3–21
Sound tab on the Frame
Properties panel.

CHECKPOINT

This would be a good time to save your work. Choose File→ Save As, and save this file in the directory of your choice as *shelley.fla*. Download the project at this point from
http://www.phptr.com/essential/flash5
or view it directly at
http://www.phptr.com/essential/flash5/shelley/shelley3-6.html.

Testing the Sound Effect

You should now have a sound when the buttons are clicked on. You can test this.

1. Choose the menu option Edit→ Edit Movie.
2. You are now presented with your current scene. Select Control→ Enable Simple Buttons.
3. Click on the last frame of your animation.
4. Move your mouse over the buttons and click on them to see the actions and hear the sound.
5. When you are through, uncheck the Control→ Enable Buttons option.

Congratulations! You have now added some basic interactivity and sound to the link buttons. This concludes the design and programming tasks needed for the Shelley project. In the next chapter, we will move on to publishing the page on the Web.

RECAP

In this chapter you've learned how to
- Create and edit symbols
- Make buttons
- Add actions and sound effects to buttons

ADVANCED PROJECTS

1. In a new movie, create several layers and use the Macromedia libraries to add symbols.
2. Open the symbol library for the current movie, and duplicate and rename a symbol. Change it to a Button symbol.
3. Insert a Get URL action for this button.
4. Change to symbol editing mode for the new button. Insert keyframes and change the appearance of the button for Up, Over, and Down.
5. Add different sounds for Over and Down, and test the button.

4 Publishing to the Web

Now that the homepage has been re-created with Flash, it's time to publish to the Web. We will start with a brief discussion of some production issues; you will need to make some decisions about how your homepage will be delivered to your audience. We will address some optimization issues. We will publish the homepage to the Web in several different formats and test them. Publishing options for your page will be discussed, and we will add preloading and plug-in detection. Finally, we will mention some Web server issues.

◆ Finishing Touches

Before we can publish our page, we need to make some decisions about the audience. Flash gives you many output options.

From providing text links for all the links in your Flash Application to producing static or animated GIFs, Flash lets you create multimedia productions while still allowing you to provide content to visitors with older browsers, low bandwidth, and fewer colors on their machines.

Deciding What Resolution to Use

The screen resolution dictates how large or small Web pages will appear. Someone with a screen resolution of 640 pixels by 480 pixels will see much less of a Web page than someone with a 1024 by 768 screen resolution. Is your audience composed of many people who view the Web in 800 by 600 resolution? Or do you want to support the lowest common denominator of your audience, which might be 640 by 480? Flash has a nice feature that will allow your page to scale with the browser. To see what this means, look at Figures 4–1 and 4–2. These are screen shots of two browser windows on the same machine. The one in Figure 4–1 has simply been reduced in size. Notice that the entire page is still visible in both windows, despite the viewable size. Your other option is to set the page as a fixed size. Viewers may need to scroll the browser window to view the entire page. This option is probably better when you are confident that your viewers are running in a higher resolution. See Figure 4–3 for an example of a tiny browser window with the Flash set to display as a fixed size.

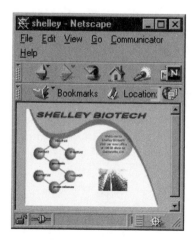

FIGURE 4–1
Screen shot with browser
window smaller.

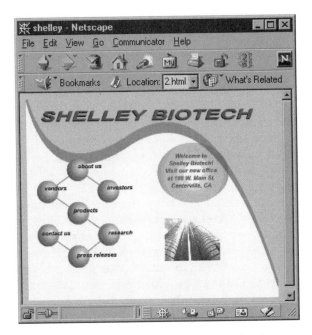

FIGURE 4–2 Screen shot with browser window larger.

FIGURE 4–3
Screen shot with Flash set to display fixed-size page.

Deciding Which Platforms to Use

Not all your visitors will view your site using Windows 98 with Internet Explorer 5. Some will use Macintoshes or Unix machines with Netscape Navigator. Some people will be using Lynx and will not be able to view your Flash movie at all. You need to decide which browsers you will support. The Flash plug-in is included with some browsers, has to be downloaded with others, and is not supported at all on some older browsers. Macromedia has a page that shows all the browsers that have a Flash plug-in available, viewable at *http://www.macromedia.com/support/flash/ts/documents/playerlocalization.htm.*

At the time of writing this book, Flash 5 is very new, and as such, most people will still need to download the Flash 5 player. Flash 5 gives you the option of publishing your movies as Flash 4 (or earlier) versions. This might be a good choice if you are concerned that your audience might choose to leave your page rather than download the new Flash 5 player. However, if your Flash 5 movie uses features only supported by the Flash 5 player, exporting your movie as Flash 4 will disable these features.

Another factor to consider is the browsers your audience will be using. One way to do this is to install a program to analyze the log files your Web server generates. If this is not a possibility for you, you can visit sites such as *http://www.browserwatch.com* to gather statistics about Web browser usage.

Deciding Which Flash Version or File Type to Use

The Flash movie file type is .swf (Shockwave Flash). However, you can generate several other types of files. If you feel that your audience will largely consist of viewers with older browsers that will not support Flash files, you can export your movie as a Java applet. You can also export your movie as an AVI or an animated GIF, but these are not useful for our purposes, because AVIs and animated GIFs created from our movie would be incredibly large files. Furthermore, the AVI would not contain the link buttons. These would not be good choices for this particular page, but a Java applet may be a good choice. In addition to allowing you many file types for exporting movies, Flash even allows you to create a standalone projector, useful for kiosk or presentation applications. The next section will describe in detail how to create pages with some of these options.

◆ Publishing

Flash 5 provides a means to create Web pages easily with your Flash movie. Flash 5 can also convert the movie file into a Java applet, as well as create the HTML code for the applet.

NOTE
You can download the project at this point from *http:// www.phptr.com/essential/flash5/shelley/shelley3-6.html.*

Choosing Format Settings

Before you can use Flash to make your Web page, you will need to specify the settings for the Shelley Biotech Flash movie and associated files. First, you need to decide which formats you will support.

1. With the most recent version of the Shelley page open, choose the menu option File→Publish Settings.
2. The Publish Settings dialog box should appear. See Figure 4–4.
3. Click on the Formats tab.
4. Uncheck the Use default names box. This allows you to rename the automatically generated files.
5. Make sure the Flash and HTML boxes are checked, but none of the others.
6. Rename the file next to the HTML box "index.html."
7. The Flash program will generate an HTML page and the movie that will be embedded in it. These will be saved in the same directory as your .fla file. Leave the dialog box open for the next set of steps.

Choosing Flash Settings

The Flash settings tab controls the way that Flash will process your movie.

1. The Publish Settings dialog box should be open. Choose the Flash tab, as shown in Figure 4–5.

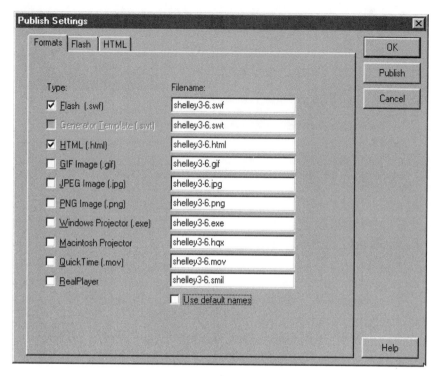

FIGURE 4–4 Publish Settings dialog box with Formats tab selected.

2. The Load Order should be Bottom Up. This controls the load order of the layers, so that the background layers will be loaded before the other layers.

3. Check the Generate Size Report box. A text file will be produced with file size information, useful for optimizing your movie. We will take a closer look at this report shortly.

4. Leave Protect from import unchecked for the purposes of this book. Leaving this unchecked allows people to download your movie from your site.

5. Leave Debugging Permitted unchecked. The debugging feature of Flash 5 is very useful, but since we only have very simple code in this movie, we won't discuss debugging until Chapter 7.

6. Set the JPEG quality to 100. Any JPEGs on the page will be uncompressed. In our case, only the office photo is affected by this setting.

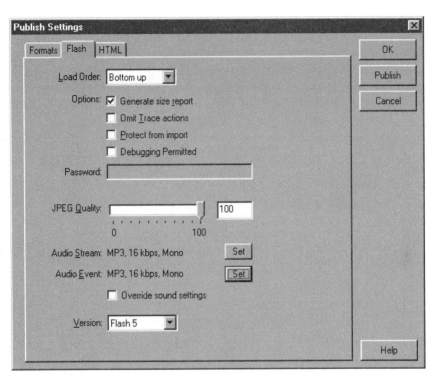

FIGURE 4-5 Publish Settings dialog box with Flash tab selected.

7. The Audio Stream settings are used to determine the quality and compression used for the streaming music on the site. Since we are not using any Audio Stream settings in this project, leave the setting disabled.

8. The Audio Event settings are used to determine the quality and compression used for the sound effects. Our buttons use sounds, so we should change this. Press the Set button and choose ADPCM for the compression, 5Khz for the rate, and 4-bit APDCM, as shown in Figure 4-6. Uncheck the Preprocessing box. Click OK.

9. Set Version as Flash 5 for now. The other options are Flash 1, Flash 2, Flash 3, and Flash 4, which are older versions of Flash. Although the Flash 5 plug-in supports these files, Flash 5 features will be disabled on movies exported as these types.

10. Do not close the dialog box. We will now change the HTML settings.

FIGURE 4–6 Sound Settings dialog box.

Choosing HTML Settings

The HTML settings tab controls the formatting of the automatically produced HTML page.

1. The Publish Settings dialog box should be open. Choose the HTML tab. See Figure 4–7.
2. Flash offers a variety of different templates. Use the Info button to find out more about each one.
3. Choose the default template, Flash Only.
4. Dimensions should be Match Movie. This will display the movie at the actual size in which we created it. If you wish the movie to scale with the window, change to Percent and specify 100 percent × 100 percent in the width and height boxes.
5. Make sure the Display Menu check box is selected. The other three Playback boxes should not be checked. The Display Menu option allows viewers to pull up a menu, as shown in Figure 4–8, using the right mouse button (PC) or Ctrl-click (Mac). The Loop box causes the movie to loop, which is not what our movie should do. Paused at Start option is also not the behavior we want. On Windows, Device font substitutes the font we chose for our text for a font already on the system viewing the movie. This can be a useful option for decreasing the size of the movie. Again, file size is not a big problem for this movie, so leave it unchecked.
6. Quality should be set to Best. The Quality option controls how the movie plays on the browser. Since Flash movies stream automatically, this affects how much anti-aliasing and smoothness the movie will contain.

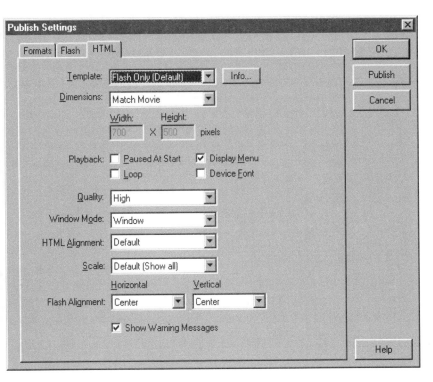

FIGURE 4–7 Publish Settings dialog box with the HTML tab selected.

FIGURE 4–8
Menu available to Flash viewers.

7. Window Mode should be set to Window. The Window option makes the movie appear in its own rectangular space on the HTML page. Opaque Windowless allows page elements to be under the movie on the page. Transparent Windowless is the same except that any transparent portions of the movie will not be visible on the page and the page elements underneath will be visible.

8. Leave both the HTML Alignment and Scale boxes set to Default.

9. Flash Alignment Horizontal and Vertical should both be set to Center. This will center the movie on the page.

10. Check the Show Warning Messages box. This will warn us of some programming problems we may have in the movie.

Publishing the Movie

You have two options for actually publishing the movie. You can click the Publish button located in the Publish Settings dialog box, or you can click OK on this dialog box and choose the menu option File→Publish. If you choose the second option, you can preview your page before actually publishing it by using the File_Publish Preview menu, and choosing the HTML option.

Viewing the Size Report

When we selected Publish settings, we instructed the program to create a size report. In the same directory as the .swf file is a file named *shelley3-6 Report.txt*. Let's take a look at each section.

Frame #	Frame Bytes	Total Bytes	Page
1	27433	27433	Scene 1
2	3035	30468	2
3	428	30896	3
4	442	31338	4
5	435	31773	5
6	447	32220	6
7	433	32653	7
8	444	33097	8
9	430	33527	9
10	444	33971	10
11	428	34399	11
12	442	34841	12
13	435	35276	13

14	449	35725	14
15	365	36090	15
16	313	36403	16
17	299	36702	17
18	313	37015	18
19	299	37314	19
20	313	37627	20
21	299	37926	21
22	313	38239	22
23	299	38538	23
24	312	38850	24
25	298	39148	25
26	312	39460	26
27	298	39758	27
28	312	40070	28
29	296	40366	29
30	1313	41679	30

Each of the frames of the animation is listed along with its size in bytes and a running total. It is important to notice that the first frame is by far the largest, and all of the following frames are tiny. This is due to the vector nature of the Flash format. The final file size is 42K. This is not incredibly large, but you'll see a way to shrink it substantially in a moment.

Page	Shape Bytes	Text Bytes
Scene 1	97	122
Embedded Objects	57	0

The Page section contains only one scene, since there is only one scene in this movie. It breaks down the number of bytes used for shapes and texts.

Symbol	Shape Bytes	Text Bytes
Photo	0	248
Address Text	0	228
Lines	60	0
Link Text	0	333
Brown Background	47	0
White Background	47	0
Link Circle	353	0

Here's a list of the symbols and their bytes. All of these are quite small. This is not where most of the size is coming from.

```
Bitmap         Compressed Original  Compression
-----------    ---------- --------- -------------
office.jpg  21727         71920     Imported JPEG
```

Here's the problem! The photograph on our page adds nearly 23K. Notice that we left the Quality set at 100 when we saved this file.

```
Tweened Shapes: 403 bytes
Event sounds: 5KHz Mono 4 bit ADPCM
Sound Name        Bytes Format
----------------- ----- --------------------
Switch Toggle     742   5KHz Mono 4 bit ADPCM
```

The sound file we used takes up a bit of space also. There is not much we can do about this, other than using the smallest possible sound files.

```
Font Name         Bytes Characters
----------------- ----- -------------------------------------
Arial             2335  ,.123EGHMOSabcefghiklnorstuwxy
Arial Bold Italic 2727  !,.01ABCEHILMOSTVWYabcdefhilmnoprstuvwy
```

This is a list of the text characters used on our page. Nearly 3K may seem a bit large, until you consider that letters can be reused without adding to this size. As long as you use the same font on the page, you can have as much text as you like without greatly increasing the size of the movie.

Optimizing the Movie

After looking over the size report, we find that the only major problem is that office photo must be uncompressed.

1. Choose Window→ Library.
2. Locate the office photo. Be careful not to select the symbol we named "Photo," but rather, the JPEG image from which it was created.
3. Choose Properties from the Options menu. See Figure 4–9.
4. Change the JPEG Quality to 30. Leave the other settings as before. Click OK.

Now let's Publish the movie and glance at the size report again. The size is now 23K! This is much better. Specifically, the photo is now around 3K in size. This will tremendously reduce

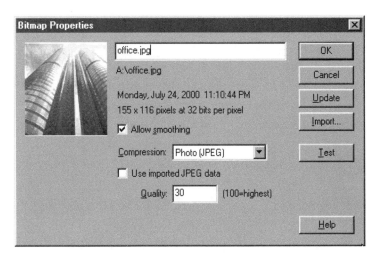

FIGURE 4–9 Bitmap Properties dialog box.

download time. If you can get by with few to no raster graphics, your movie will be much more compact.

It's time to publish our movie to the Web. While Flash is an extremely robust application offering you many options for producing your movie, there may be times when you do not want to use it to create the HTML. Perhaps you don't have it available, or you simply wish to gain an understanding of the HTML code necessary to play your movie. This section offers you some insight on the HTML side of things. You are assumed to have a basic knowledge of HTML tags. Tags that are not specifically discussed are common HTML tags that you can look up in an HTML reference.

Writing the HTML for the .swf File

When you saved your movie from the Flash 5 program, you named it *shelley3-6.swf*. To generate only a movie and no HTML files, you need to uncheck the HTML box on the Formats tab of the Publish Settings dialog box. The code you would need to publish this to an HTML file follows, along with a discussion of the various tags specific to the Flash files.

```
<HTML>
<HEAD>
<TITLE>Shelley Biotech</TITLE>
</HEAD>
<BODY bgcolor="#CCCC99">
```

This `bgcolor` matches our movie. You will need to add the text and link colors you want, unless the browser defaults are sufficient.

```
<OBJECT classid=
"clsid:D27CDB6E-AE6D-11cf-96B8-444553540000"
ID=shelley WIDTH=100% HEIGHT=100%>
```

The `OBJECT` tag is used for Internet Explorer to allow the Flash to be embedded as an Active X control. This is necessary only if you wish to allow your Flash movie to be viewable on an IE browser with a Flash Active X control. The `classid` value identifies the specific Active X control to use. The `WIDTH` and `HEIGHT` tags are responsible for making the Active X control match the browser size. This can be hardwired as a specific pixel size by removing the % sign and changing these values. It is somewhat unlikely that you will need to ever present your movies with an Active X control, as later versions of the browsers have the Flash Player included. The only time you might need to do this is if for some reason you are designing movies for an environment with earlier IE versions and no Flash plug-ins.

```
<PARAM NAME=movie VALUE="shelley3-6.swf">
```

The `PARAM` tags tell the Flash player how the movie should be displayed. This first one points at the .swf file to use.

```
<PARAM NAME=loop VALUE=false>
```

This `PARAM` tag tells the Flash player to play this file a single time and then to stop. If you wished the file to loop indefinitely, you would set this to true.

```
<PARAM NAME=quality VALUE=high>
```

The quality `PARAM` tag tells the Flash player to display this movie with high image quality, sacrificing speed for quality. To make the movie play at the highest quality no matter what, set this to best.

```
<PARAM NAME=bgcolor VALUE=#CCCC99>
```

The background color of the Flash player area should match the page background and the movie background.

```
<EMBED SRC="shelley3-6.swf" WIDTH=100% HEIGHT=100%
LOOP=false
QUALITY=high
BGCOLOR=#CCCC99
TYPE="application/x-shockwave-flash" >
```

The EMBED tag is used to call the Flash player and tell it how to play the movie.

```
</EMBED>
</OBJECT>
</BODY>
</HTML>
```

Creating a Non-Flash Version of the Page

Flash provides a means for creating static pages from your Flash movie. Flash can create a static GIF with an image map from one of the frames from your Flash movie.

1. Select the frame in your movie of which you wish to create a static GIF. In the case of the Shelley site, it should be the last frame, frame 30.
2. Click on the thirtieth frame of the top layer. Choose Window→ Panels→ Frame.
3. Enter "#Static" in the Label blank. See Figure 4–10. This label tells Flash which frame to use.
4. With the current version of the Shelley page, choose File→ Publish Settings.
5. Select the Formats tab. Check the box next to GIF Image. See Figure 4–11.
6. Now select the HTML tab. Choose Image Map from the Template list box, as shown in Figure 4–12.
7. Choose the GIF tab and use the settings shown in Figure 4–13.

FIGURE 4–10
Frame Properties panel.

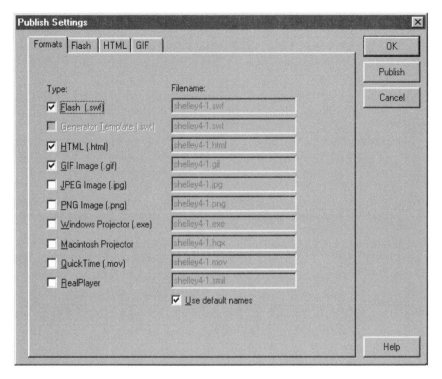

FIGURE 4–11 Publish Settings dialog box with Formats tab selected.

8. Click Publish and then click OK. Use File→Publish Preview to view the various files that Flash will create with the chosen settings. Keep in mind that GIF images have palettes limited to 256 colors or less, so any photos or gradient fills on your page will be dithered.

CHECKPOINT
This would be a good time to save your work. Choose File→ Save As, and save this file in the directory of your choice as *shelley.fla*. Download the project at this point from
http://www.phptr.com/essential/flash5
or view it directly at
http://www.phptr.com/essential/flash5/shelley/shelley4-1.html.

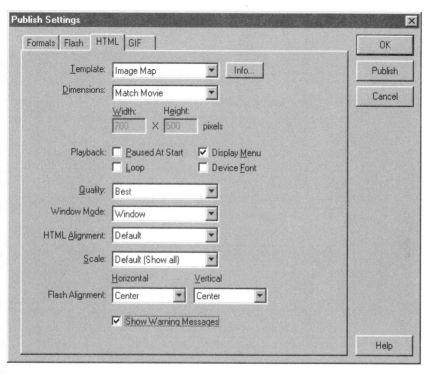

FIGURE 4–12 Publish Settings dialog box with HTML tab selected.

A Few Final Web Publishing Issues

If you use Flash to create your HTML file, you may have to hand-edit the HTML file produced, should you FTP or otherwise move this file. Flash may put hard paths to files in the code that will need to be changed to reflect the move. Also make sure that the appropriate Java files reside in the specified directory for any Java applets you produce and move. Finally, Flash may produce more than an HTML file, so make sure you move the .html, .swf, and all other files associated with your page to the appropriate directory. An example of this is when you tell Flash to produce a static GIF file for browsers with no Flash support. Flash creates a .gif file as well as the .html.

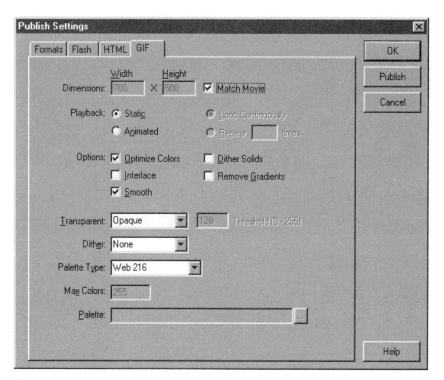

FIGURE 4–13 Publish Settings dialog box with GIF tab selected.

◆ Preloading

Preloading is a technique used to let the viewer know the page is being loaded. Instead of a blank page being presented to the viewer, a graphic can be used to indicate that loading is taking place. This section will explain how to add a simple preload scene to the Shelley page.

Adding a Scene to the Current Movie

1. Open the current *shelley.fla* or download and open *shelley4-1.fla*.
2. Choose Insert→ Scene. You are now presented with a new blank scene. To change the current scene, use the Scene List button, shown just above frame 24 in Figure 4–14.
3. Open the Scene Panel, shown in Figure 4–15, by choosing Window→ Panels→ Scene.

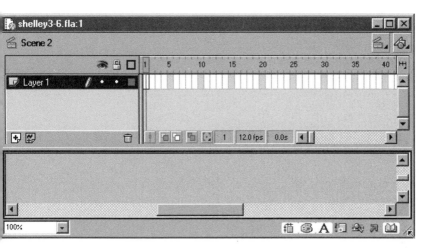

FIGURE 4–14 New blank scene.

4. Highlight Scene 1 in this panel. Scene 1 is the scene with the graphics and animation.
5. Double-click on its name and change it to "Main" and press Enter. See Figure 4–16.

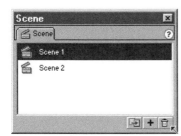

FIGURE 4–15
Scene panel.

FIGURE 4–16
Scene panel.

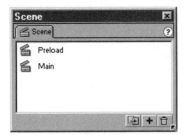

FIGURE 4–17
Scene panel.

6. Highlight Scene 2 in this panel. Scene 2 is the blank scene we just added.
7. Change its name to "Preload" and press Enter.
8. Finally, the order of the scenes needs to be changed. Click and drag the Preload label above the Main label, as shown in Figure 4–17. Now the Preload scene will play, followed by the Main scene.

Modifying the Preload Scene

1. Make sure the currently selected scene is the Preload scene.
2. Choose Insert→ Layer. This scene now has two layers.
3. Rename the top layer "Tags."
4. Rename the bottom layer "Actions."
5. Click on Frame 1 in the Tags layer. Open the Frame panel.
6. Select the Label tab, shown in Figure 4–18.
7. Type "Begin" for the label name.

Creating the Preloading Animation

1. Click on keyframe 1 of the Actions layer.
2. Select the Text tool and type the words "Page Loading," using Arial for the font, black for the color, and 48 for the size.

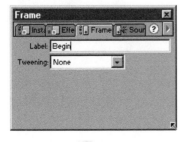

FIGURE 4–18
Frame panel.

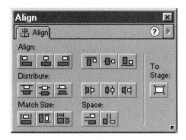

FIGURE 4–19
Align panel.

3. Move the text with the Arrow to the center of the scene. You may want to use the Align panel to center it. See Figure 4–19.
4. Select this text and choose Insert→ Convert to Symbol.
5. Name this symbol "Loading" and choose Graphic for behavior. Click OK.
6. Insert a keyframe at frame 10 for both the Tags and Actions layers.
7. Click on keyframe 10 of the Actions layer. We will make the loading text fade out.
8. Select the Page Loading text and open the Effects panel.
9. Choose Alpha from the list box and move the slider to 0%. See Figure 4–20.
10. To add Tweening, click on the first keyframe. Open the Frame panel.
11. Choose Motion from the Tweening drop-down box. See Figure 4–21.

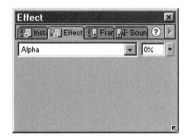

FIGURE 4–20
Effects panel.

FIGURE 4–21
Frame panel.

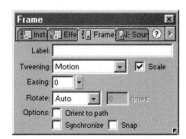

Adding the Action Code

The only thing left to do is to add the code to tell the preloader when to quit playing.

1. Select the first keyframe in the Actions layer of the Preload scene.
2. Double-click this keyframe to open the Frame Actions dialog.
3. Click on Basic Actions and double-click on If Frame Is Loaded in the menu. See Figure 4–22.
4. On the bottom of this dialog, choose Main from the Scene drop-down box.
5. Select Frame Number from the Type drop-down and type 30 in the Frame box.
6. Now double-click Go To from the Basic Actions. See Figure 4–23.

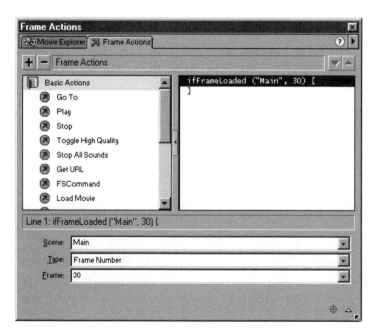

FIGURE 4–22 Frame Actions dialog box.

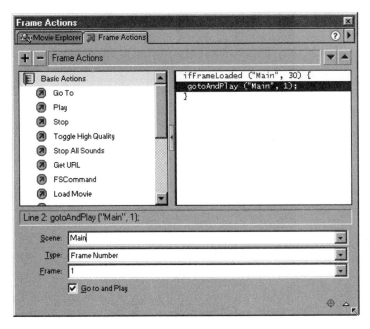

FIGURE 4–23 Frame Actions dialog box.

7. On the bottom of this dialog, choose Main from the Scene drop-down box.

8. Select Frame Number from the Type drop-down and type 1 in the Frame box.

We have just told the Preload scene to play until frame 30 of the Main scene is loaded. The only problem is that the Preload scene will only play once. We need to make it loop until the frame is loaded. To do this:

1. Make sure the Go to and Play check box is selected. Close this dialog.

2. Double-click on the keyframe at frame 10 of the Actions layer. This opens the Frame Actions dialog again.

3. Double-click on Go To from the Basic Actions menu. See Figure 4–24.

4. For the Scene option on the bottom, choose Preload.

5. Select the "Frame Label" option for Type and choose Begin from the Frame list box.

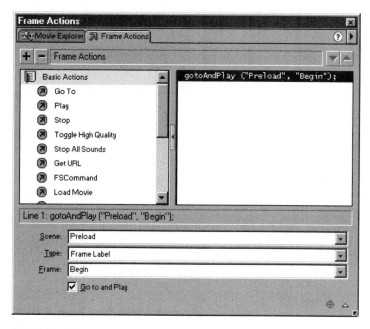

FIGURE 4–24 Frame Actions dialog box.

6. Make sure the Go to and Play check box is selected. Close this dialog.

Putting in a Stop Action

The last thing we need to do is add a Stop action to the Main scene. Without this in place, the movie will loop.

1. Use the Scene List button to change to the Main scene.
2. Select the final keyframe of any layer. The example file uses the Header Text layer.
3. Double-click on this keyframe to open the Frame Actions dialog.
4. Choose Stop from the Basic Actions menu in this dialog. Close the dialog.

That's it. You now have a very simple preloader that will play the loading animation until the final frame of the movie is loaded. To preview your movie, choose Control→ Test Movie. You will probably not see the preloader scene using this, as all the graphics are already in memory and quickly accessed. You can also use the File→Publish Preview option to test it out, and the File→Publish option to create a final version. You may need to actually upload your HTML and .swf files to a Web server to slow down the loading enough for the preloader to be noticeable.

◆ Detecting the Plug-In

Several techniques are used to manage detection of the Flash plug-in. The simplest involve self-selection; the most complex use scripting languages. This section will discuss the reasoning behind using one over another and will provide you with a scheme for using Flash to accomplish plug-in detection.

The simplest technique is to allow the user to self-select. In this scenario, the user is presented with a basic HTML page with a link for both a Flash version and a non-Flash version of the site. This assumes that users know whether or not they have the plug-in. Many average users probably do not know, so this is not necessarily the best choice.

Building on the idea of self-selection, the users may again be presented with a choice, but this time a small Flash movie can be embedded in the page. The page should point out to the users that they should enter the Flash site if they can see the animation in the movie. In both cases, it's a good idea to put in links to Macromedia's site and to give instructions on getting the plug-in.

Flash has a template under the Publish Settings menu that does this for you. You may have to hand-edit the page to add the appropriate text for your particular page. Using JavaScript to detect the plug-in has definite advantages. The user does not have to make any choices and can be automatically pointed to the appropriate page. The main disadvantage to using JavaScript is that the scripts tend to be long and complicated. If you decide to use it, you should search on the Web for scripts already written for this purpose. A good place to look is *http://www.FlashCentral.com/Tech/Detect/*.

The best middle-of-the-road approach to detecting the plug-in is to use Flash. Since Flash supports frame actions, a small movie on a page can be directed to load another page when it hits a specific frame. Only browsers with the plug-in installed will be able to execute the command.

Modifying the Movie for Flash Detection

1. Choose File→ New.
2. Open the Movie Properties dialog box by choosing Modify→ Movie.
3. Change the movie to the smallest allowable size, 18 pixels × 18 pixels. See Figure 4–25.
4. Change the background color to match your page. This is the light tan color in the eleventh column and third row from the bottom, as shown in Figure 4–26. Click OK.
5. Choose the Layer 1 keyframe at frame 1.
6. Double-click this frame to open the Frame Actions dialog.
7. Select the Actions tab, shown in Figure 4–27.
8. Choose Get URL from the Basic Actions menu and enter the appropriate URL in the blank on the bottom. This will be the location of the Flash version of the site.
9. Choose _self from the Window list box. If you want to load the Flash site in another window, use _blank. Close this dialog.

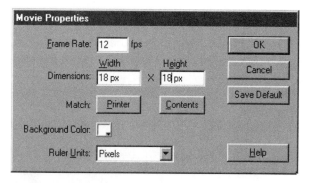

FIGURE 4–25 Movie Properties dialog box.

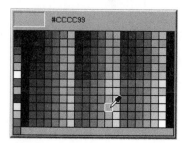

FIGURE 4–26
Color palette.

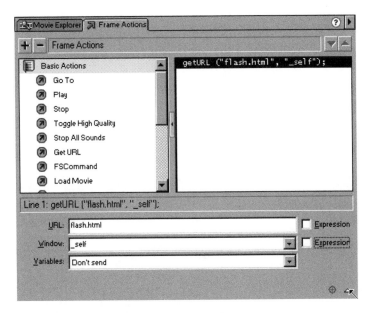

FIGURE 4–27 Frame Actions dialog box.

10. Choose File→ Publish Settings. Under the Formats tab, only the Flash check box should be selected. See Figure 4–28.
11. Uncheck the Use Default Names box and type the name "detect.swf" next to the Flash check box.
12. Click Publish and click OK.

Creating the HTML Page for This Movie

The movie we just created needs to be embedded in an HTML page. The source code that follows demonstrates a page that sends browsers without the plug-in to another page after several seconds.

```
<HTML>
<HEAD>
<TITLE>Shelley Biotech Flash Site</TITLE>
<!—The Meta statement below automatically redirects non-
flash enabled
browsers to index2.html, a static version of the Shelley
page. --!>
<META HTTP-EQUIV="Refresh" CONTENT="15;
URL=index2.html">
</HEAD>
```

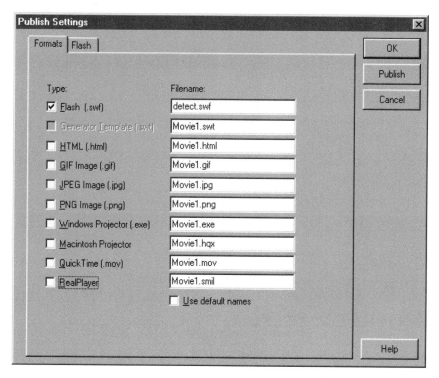

FIGURE 4–28 Publish Settings dialog box with Formats tab selected.

```
<BODY BGCOLOR="# CCCC99">
<OBJECT CLASSID="clsid:D27CDB6E-AE6D-11cf-96B8-
444553540000"
WIDTH=" HEIGHT=" CODEBASE="http://active.macromedia.com/
flash3/cabs/">
<PARAM NAME="MOVIE" VALUE="detect.swf">
<PARAM NAME="PLAY" VALUE="true">
<PARAM NAME="LOOP" VALUE="false">
<PARAM NAME="QUALITY" VALUE="high">
<PARAM NAME="SCALE" VALUE="SHOWALL">
<EMBED SRC="shelley.swf" WIDTH="18" HEIGHT="18"
PLAY="true"
LOOP="false" QUALITY="high" SCALE="SHOWALL"
PLUGINSPAGE="http://www.macromedia.com/shockwave/download
/index.cgi?P1_Prod_Version=ShockwaveFlash">
</EMBED>
</OBJECT>
</BODY>
</HTML>
```

◆ Web Server Settings

Before a Flash movie can be viewed on the Web, the Web server must know how to deliver it. Web servers have configuration files with a list of MIME (Multipurpose Internet Mail Extensions) types. When a Web server receives a request for a file with a listed MIME type, it sends a file descriptor, followed by the requested file. The browser then knows which plug-in to use to display the file. If the Web server is correctly configured, you will be able to upload your files into your Web directory and be able to view them correctly in a browser with the correct Flash plug-in. If you can't view the file, or the Web server sends you a text page, you should contact your Internet Service Provider's system administrator or technical support person and ask that the Web server's MIME types be modified to send Flash 5 correctly. If you manage your own Web server, brief instructions for modifying some of the more common Web servers follow.

Configuring Apache

1. Locate the mime.types file in your Apache conf/ directory.
2. Edit this file and add the line:

```
application/x-shockwave-flash swf
```

3. Save the file and restart the Apache server.

Configuring IIS 4.0

1. Choose from the Start menu Programs→ Windows NT 4.0 Option Pack→ Microsoft Internet Information Server→ Internet Service Manager.
2. From the Console dialog box, select Console Root→ Internet Information Server→ Your Computer.
3. Right-click on Your Computer.
4. Choose Properties from the menu.
5. Click the File Types button.
6. In the File Type dialog box, type ".swf" as an Associated Extension.
7. For Content Type, type "application/x-shockwave-flash."
8. Click OK on all of the dialog boxes.

For other Web servers, view the help documents for instructions on inserting MIME types. The specific information needed by all servers is

```
MIME Type: application/x-shockwave-flash Suffix: .swf
```

In this chapter we have finished the Shelley Biotech homepage by publishing it to the Web. This project touched on many of the basic features of Flash. The second half of this book will focus on building a more elaborate Flash project, with a greater emphasis on interactivity and multimedia.

RECAP

In this chapter you've learned how to:

- Publish a Flash movie to the Web in different formats
- Preload a Flash movie
- Detect the Flash plug-In
- Set up a Web server for Flash

ADVANCED PROJECTS

1. Change the static GIF Flash produces to a different frame.
2. Try publishing the Shelley page with different Template options from the HTML tab of the Publish Settings dialog box and test the results on different browsers.
3. Change the browser detection method.

5 Fine-Tuning Graphics

*T*he next three chapters will be devoted to developing the Stitch site. Stitch is an online fashion magazine with some bells and whistles the Shelley Biotech site did not have. The Stitch site has an animated splash screen, a Flash-based menuing system, a contact form, and an interactive fashion show. In this chapter, you will learn some more advanced graphic techniques, including modification of basic shapes and intersections. You will use these techniques to create the animated Stitch Web site splash screen.

◆ Reshaping

Drawing shapes freehand to achieve the effect you desire can be very difficult. It is often easier to draw a rough approximation of

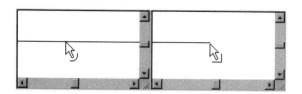

FIGURE 5–1 Adding curves to lines and moving endpoints of lines.

the desired shape and then manipulate it into the final image. Flash provides two very simple ways to modify shapes and lines.

So far, you have used the Arrow tool to select, resize, rotate, and move graphic objects. It is also used to reshape graphics. To try it out, open Flash and draw something. Switch to the Arrow tool. Do not click on the graphic, but instead move the cursor to the edge of the graphic. The cursor will change to look like one of the two cursors shown in Figure 5–1. At this point, if you click, hold, and drag the edge of your graphic, you will reshape it. The curve under the arrow means that you will be moving a curve, the angle means that you are at a corner or endpoint.

Flash 5 also provides a Bezier tool for shaping graphics. If you are comfortable using beziers to shape graphics, click on the Subselect tool, which is the white arrow on the toolbar. Then click on the edge of your graphic. You will see a blue outline with specific points. Click on any point on a curve to highlight it and use the two handles that appear next to it to change the curve.

In this section, you will be creating and reshaping graphics for the splash screen. For the splash screen, we will be using a dark blue background with white and gray graphics and text. A preview of the splash screen is shown in Figure 5–2.

Getting Started

1. Start the Flash program. A new blank movie should appear.
2. Choose Modify→ Movie.
3. Change the background color to the dark blue in the third column of the second row, as shown in Figure 5–3.
4. Change the size of the movie to 600 px × 500 px.
5. Set the frame rate to 12 fps.
6. Choose View→ Grid→ Edit Grid.
7. Change the grid spacing to 10 px by 10 px. Select OK.

FIGURE 5–2 Splash screen.

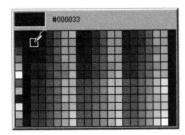

FIGURE 5–3
Movie Properties dialog box with
the background color palette.

CHECKPOINT

This would be a good time to save your work. Choose File→ Save As, and save this file in the directory of your choice as *stitch.fla*. Download the project at this point from
http://www.phptr.com/essential/flash5
or view it directly at
http://www.phptr.com/essential/flash5/stitch/stitch5-1.html.

Drawing the Needle Graphic

Looking back at Figure 5–2, you will notice a sewing needle graphic. The steps that follow describe how to draw the outline of the needle, as seen in Figure 5–4.

1. Begin by making the grid visible by choosing View→ Grid→ Show Grid.
2. Select the View→ Grid→ Snap to Grid option.
3. You may want to change the grid color to a darker one to allow you to see more clearly the image you will be creating. Select View→ Grid→ Edit Grid and change the grid color to a dark gray.
4. Change to the Oval tool. Use the Stroke panel to change the line color to white, thickness to 1.0, and style solid.

FIGURE 5–4
Outline of needle.

FIGURE 5–5
Oval tool settings.

5. Make the fill transparent by clicking on Fill Color on the Tools menu and clicking on the button with the white square with the red diagonal line just below it, shown in Figure 5–5.
6. Draw an oval.
7. Select the oval you just created and use the Info panel to change it to approximately 300 px in height and 40 px in width.
8. Change to the Arrow tool.

We are now going to change the shape of this oval to the needle outline. You will be reshaping the outline. You can use both the Select tool and the Subselect tool to do this. We'll use the Select tool in the steps below.

1. Move your arrow over the oval outline on the left side near the center, as shown in Figure 5–6. With the arrow cursor changed to look like the one in the image, hold

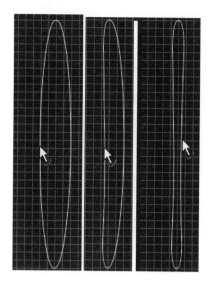

FIGURE 5-6
Reshape the oval.

down the mouse button and drag the outline toward the center of the oval until it resembles the figure. Do the same thing for the right side.

2. Next, we need to make the point of the needle. On the outline at approximately 20 pixels from the bottom of the oval, click, hold, and drag the outline toward the center line on each side, as shown in Figure 5-7.

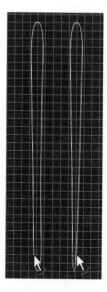

FIGURE 5-7
Create the point of the needle.

3. The last step is to add the eye of the needle. Select the Oval tool. The options should still be the same as those you used for drawing the needle outline.

4. Turn off View→ Grid→ Snap to Grid. Make sure View→ Snap to Objects is off as well.

5. Near the upper part of the needle, draw a tall thin circle for the eye. If you need to adjust this circle, change to the Arrow tool and click on it to select it. You can then move it or reshape it as necessary.

CHECKPOINT
This would be a good time to save your work. Choose File→ Save As, and save this file in the directory of your choice as *stitch.fla*. Download the project at this point from
http://www.phptr.com/essential/flash5
or view it directly at
http://www.phptr.com/essential/flash5/stitch/stitch5-2.html.

Filling in Needle Texture

Now that you have drawn the needle outline, it's time to fill it with a texture.

1. Choose the Paint Bucket.
2. Open the Fill panel. Choose Linear Gradient from the drop-down menu on this panel.
3. We are going to create a new linear gradient. We need to change the two color markers on the Fill panel. See Figure 5–8.
4. Click on the left color marker. Notice that the Mixer panel now displays this marker, as shown in Figure 5–9.

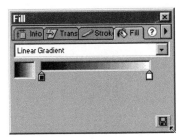

FIGURE 5–8
Fill panel.

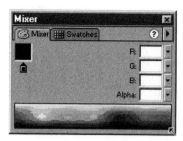

FIGURE 5–9
Mixer panel.

5. In the Mixer panel, change the color on the left to have RGB values of 200, 200, 200. Click on the right color marker in the Fill panel and change it in the Mixer panel to 45, 45, 45.
6. Let's save the new gradient. On the Fill panel, click on the small black arrow to the right of the question mark. Select Add Gradient. The texture should now be selected for the Paint Bucket tool.
7. Use the Paint Bucket and click inside the needle outline to fill it.
8. Change to the Arrow tool. Select the white outlines and delete them.

Tilting the Needle

We need to rotate the needle to a more pleasing angle.

1. Change to the Arrow.
2. Select the needle.
3. Click on the Rotate option near the bottom of the tool palette.
4. Click, hold, and move one of the corner handles until the needle angle resembles Figure 5–10.

CHECKPOINT
This would be a good time to save your work. Choose File→ Save As, and save this file in the directory of your choice as *stitch.fla*. Download the project at this point from
http://www.phptr.com/essential/flash5
or view it directly at
http://www.phptr.com/essential/flash5/stitch/stitch5-3.html.

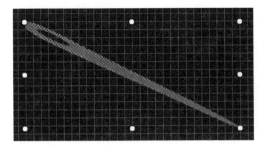

FIGURE 5–10 Tilted needle.

Drawing the Thread

Now we will draw the thread that hangs from the needle.

1. You will need a new layer for the thread. Choose the Insert Layer option from the Layers menu. Name the new layer "Thread." You should also change the name of Layer 1 to "Needle."
2. Hide the grid by unchecking View→ Grid→ Show Grid.
3. Make sure the Thread layer is currently selected. Choose the Pencil tool.
4. The pencil settings should be changed on the Stroke panel, as seen in Figure 5–11. The pencil color should be white, a thickness of 2.0, and the style should be dashed. Also, change the Pencil Mode to Smooth under the Tools Options.
5. Draw two wavy lines from the eye of the needle to resemble those in Figure 5–12. You do not have to draw them exactly as you want them to look. You can change to the Arrow tool and reshape them. It is very easy to modify and lengthen the lines with the Arrow tool.

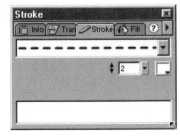

FIGURE 5–11
Pencil settings.

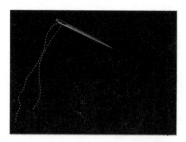

FIGURE 5–12
Needle with thread.

6. Move the needle and thread lines approximately to the locations shown in Figure 5–12.

◆ Intersections

In addition to reshaping, Flash offers another useful feature for creating custom images. A graphic can be subtracted from another graphic. Basically, this means that you can create images with holes in them. This is accomplished by creating two graphics in the same layer, dragging one on top of the other, and then deleting the top one. For example, if you want to make a doughnut shape, you can create two filled circles, one much larger than the other, and then move the smaller one to the center of the large one and deselect both. Finally, select the small circle and delete it, and you are left with a large filled circle with a hole in it. As soon as the top one is deselected, it erases anything that was underneath it. It can then be moved or deleted, and empty space remains. Also, if the top graphic went all the way across the bottom one, the bottom one is now in two separate pieces. Figure 5–13 should make this clearer. This image shows two objects and the results of deleting the top one, and also the components that result from their intersection. In the next steps, we will use intersection to create the button image, create the *Stitch* text, and add the image.

Creating the Button Texture

The button texture consists of a gradient fill with three colors. Figure 5–14 shows the Fill panel with the gradient. To create this texture:

1. Select the Fill panel.

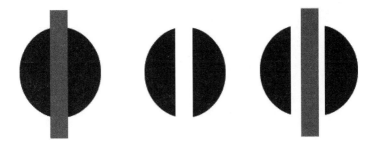

FIGURE 5–13 Intersecting two shapes.

2. Choose Radial Gradient from the drop-down list.
3. You now should see two color markers. We actually want three color markers. To add one, click on the color bar midway between the right and left markers. If you accidentally add too many, click on the excess marker and drag downwards Click and drag the three markers to the same approximate locations as shown in Figure 5–14.
4. Click on each color marker and notice it show up in the Mixer panel. The RGB values of the three, from left to right, are 255, 255, 255(white), 193, 193, 193 (black), and 0, 0, 51 (dark blue). Use the Mixer panel to change them.
5. Save this new gradient by clicking on the small black arrow on the Fill panel to the right of the question mark and choosing Add Gradient.
6. Create a new layer by choosing Insert→ Layer. Name it "Button."
7. Select the Button layer and hide the others with the Layers menu. Remember, you can open the Layers menu by right-clicking (PC) or ctrl-clicking (Mac) on the Layer names.

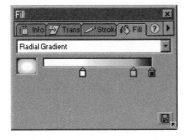

FIGURE 5–14
Fill panel.

FIGURE 5–15
Oval tool and settings.

8. Use the Oval tool with the options shown in Figure 5–15. Set the Line color to transparent under the Tools Colors menu on the left. The Fill color should be the one we just created.

9. Draw a circle of any size. Select it and use the Info panel to change it to a 70 height by 70 width pixel circle. See Figure 5–16.

FIGURE 5–16
Circle with new fill.

CHECKPOINT

This would be a good time to save your work. Choose File→ Save As, and save this file in the directory of your choice as *stitch.fla*. Download the project at this point from
http://www.phptr.com/essential/flash5
or view it directly at
http://www.phptr.com/essential/flash5/stitch/stitch5-4.html.

Creating the Buttonholes

We will now use intersection to create the buttonholes, then add small objects to give the illusion of thread. Figure 5–17 shows the button and the approximate size of the buttonholes you need to create.

1. Select Button as the current layer. IMPORTANT, make sure the Button is NOT selected!
2. Change to the Oval tool. Using the Fill and Line colors on the left under the Tools menu, select a light gray Fill color and set the Line color to transparent, as shown in Figure 5–18.
3. Draw a small oval, as shown in Figure 5–17.
4. Select the oval and choose Edit→ Copy.
5. Choose Edit→ Paste to place a new copy of the oval.
6. Select and move the copy next to the original, as shown. It may be helpful to select both images and use the Align panel.
7. Select both ovals and place them in the center of the button. Do not deselect them until you have placed them exactly where they need to go.
8. To create the intersection, simply deselect all by clicking on a blank part of the work area. Move the button to the side. It will now have the buttonholes in it.
9. Select and delete the two ovals.

FIGURE 5–17
Buttonholes and button.

FIGURE 5-18
Oval tool and settings.

CHECKPOINT

This would be a good time to save your work. Choose File→ Save As, and save this file in the directory of your choice as *stitch.fla.* Download the project at this point from
http://www.phptr.com/essential/flash5
or view it directly at
http://www.phptr.com/essential/flash5/stitch/stitch5-5.html.

Adding the Thread Fill to the Buttonholes

1. To add the thread illusion, you will need a new texture. Choose the Paint Bucket and open the Fill panel. Make sure nothing on the stage is selected.

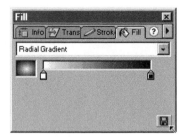

FIGURE 5–19
Fill panel.

2. Choose Radial Gradient from the drop-down list. The gradient that is presented is the one we created earlier. See Figure 5–19.
3. The new gradient fill needs only two color markers. Move two of the markers to either end of the bar and click, hold, and drag down with the third to get rid of it. The two markers should go from white (255, 255, 255) on the left to the same dark blue as the background (0, 0, 51) on the right. Click each and change its color in the Mixer panel.
4. Save this new gradient by clicking on the small black arrow on the Fill panel to the right of the question mark and choosing Add Gradient.
5. Using the Paint Bucket tool, click in the center of each of the buttonholes to fill with this texture.
6. Your button should now look like Figure 5–20.
7. Select the button and buttonholes at the same time and choose Modify→ Group.

CHECKPOINT
This would be a good time to save your work. Choose File→ Save As, and save this file in the directory of your choice as *stitch.fla*. Download the project at this point from
http://www.phptr.com/essential/flash5
or view it directly at
http://www.phptr.com/essential/flash5/stitch/stitch5-6.html.

FIGURE 5–20
Button with filled buttonholes.

Now that you have created the needle, thread, and button, you should add the main title text and begin placing objects on the page. The font used in the *Stitch* example is Impact, but many other fonts could be used in its place. It was chosen because it is a very bold font.

Creating the Text

The text on the splash screen consists of the title, the subtitle, and the article teaser.

1. Make sure View→Antialias Text is checked.
2. Create a new layer and name it "Text." Right-click (PC) or Ctrl-click (Mac) on this layer to open the Layers Menu and hide the others.
3. Select the Text tool. Open the Character panel. Choose Impact or something similar for the font, white for the color, and 48 for the size.
4. Click on the scene and add the text "Stitch." At this point the size does not matter; we can resize it later if necessary. Deselect the text. See Figure 5–21.

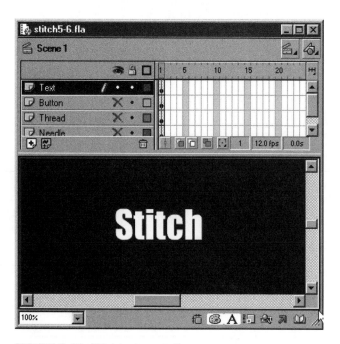

FIGURE 5–21 *Stitch* text created.

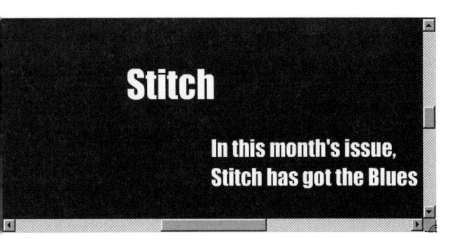

FIGURE 5–22 "Blues" text added.

5. Change to a font size of 28. Click on a different area of the screen and type the text as shown in Figure 5–22: "In this month's issue, Stitch has got the Blues." Put a carriage return after the comma. Deselect the text.
6. Highlight just the word "Blues" with the Text cursor, as shown in Figure 5–23.
7. Click on the color palette on the Character panel and select a light blue color. The example site is using RGB 51, 153, 204. Click somewhere else on the scene.

FIGURE 5–23 Blues text with the word "Blues" highlighted.

FIGURE 5–24 "Fashion Journal" text added.

8. Now use the Character panel to change the font size to 48 and the color to medium gray.
9. Type the text "Fashion Journal." See Figure 5–24.
10. Change to the Arrow. Click on the *Stitch* text to select it.
11. On the Info panel, resize the text to approximately 500 px wide by 90 px high, as shown in Figure 5–25.
12. Choose Show All from the Layers menu.
13. The other two text objects do not need to be resized. Move all the graphics to the appropriate locations, as seen in Figure 5–26.

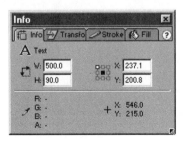

FIGURE 5–25
Info panel.

FIGURE 5-26 Graphics moved to final locations.

CHECKPOINT

This would be a good time to save your work. Choose File→ Save As, and save this file in the directory of your choice as *stitch.fla.* Download the project at this point from
http://www.phptr.com/essential/flash5
or view it directly at
http://www.phptr.com/essential/flash5/stitch/stitch5-7.html.

Coloring the Text

To add a little more visual interest to the *Stitch* text, we will add the same gradient fill as was used for the button graphic. Since text objects can't be given gradient fills, we will convert it to a nontext graphic. The text before and after the fill is applied is shown in Figure 5-27. The difference is subtle.

FIGURE 5–27 Unfilled and filled *Stitch*.

1. Turn off the grid if it is on. Hide all layers except the Text layer.
2. Select the *Stitch* text. Make sure nothing else is currently selected.
3. Choose the menu option Modify➔ Break Apart.
4. Deselect the text.
5. Change to the Paint Bucket. Click on the Fill color palette button under Colors on the Tools menu, located on the left. Select the gradient you used for the button fill. Since we saved it earlier, it will appear at the bottom of the color palette.
6. Click on the center area of each letter to apply the fill. You will have to treat the dot above the letter *i* as a separate object.
7. Change to the Arrow tool and, holding down the Shift key, select all the pieces. Choose Modify➔ Group. This will group the text.

CHECKPOINT

This would be a good time to save your work. Choose File➔ Save As, and save this file in the directory of your choice as *stitch.fla*. Download the project at this point from
http://www.phptr.com/essential/flash5
or view it directly at
http://www.phptr.com/essential/flash5/stitch/stitch5-8.html.

Adding the Photographic Image

The photo used on this page was edited in a different graphics program so that it would have the same background color as the page.

1. This image can be downloaded from the Web at *http://www.phptr.com/essential/flash5/stitch/misc/splash.jpg.*
2. Make sure all the layers are showing by choosing Show All from the Layers menu. Create and select a new layer called "Photo." Make sure this layer is selected.
3. Select File➔ Import and select the image from wherever you saved it.
4. Use the Arrow to select and move the image to its appropriate location. See Figure 5–28.
5. Change the layer order to Button, Thread, Text, Needle, Photo.

CHECKPOINT

This would be a good time to save your work. Choose File➔ Save As, and save this file in the directory of your choice as *stitch.fla*. Download the project at this point from
http://www.phptr.com/essential/flash5
or view it directly at
http://www.phptr.com/essential/flash5/stitch/stitch5-9.html.

FIGURE 5–28 Photograph imported and moved.

◆ Brush Effects

The Brush tool is very powerful for creating freehand graphics. On this splash page, it is used for the free-form shadows from the photo and the button.

Creating the Shadow for the Button and Photo

1. Create a new layer and call it "Shadows." Make sure it is selected.
2. Click and drag the Shadows layer above the Photo layer if it is not already there.
3. Change to the Brush tool.
4. Choose Paint Normal for the Brush Mode under Options. Choose the fifth brush size in the list, shown in Figure 5–29.
5. Use the round brush shape. Use black for the Fill color. See Figure 5–30.

FIGURE 5–29
The brush-size list.

FIGURE 5–30
Brush tool with settings.

FIGURE 5–31 Model photograph with shadow.

6. Make sure you are in the Shadows layer.
7. Draw a shadow shape next to the button.
8. Draw a shadow shape next to the photo. Figures 5–31 and 5–32 show the shadows against a white movie background so you can see the shapes more clearly. The edges will be softened later.

CHECKPOINT
This would be a good time to save your work. Choose File→ Save As, and save this file in the directory of your choice as *stitch.fla*. Download the project at this point from
http://www.phptr.com/essential/flash5
or view it directly at
http://www.phptr.com/essential/flash5/stitch/stitch5-10.html.

The shadow may be too long, or it may have edges that should be smoothed. Brush shapes can be treated just like any other shapes in Flash. To modify the size, select the shadow and use the Scale and Rotate buttons to make the desired changes. To change the edges, deselect the shadow. Move the mouse cursor to the edge that you wish to modify. When the cursor changes, click and drag the edge to modify it.

FIGURE 5–32
Button with shadow.

Creating Gradient for Shadows

We should give the shadows a softer edge. In Flash 4, you would have created a new gradient fill with a semi-transparent color at the edges. Flash 5 give us a much simpler way to do this.

1. Select the shadow we added for the button.
2. Choose Modify➔ Shape➔ Soften Fill Edges.
3. This opens the Soften Edges dialog, shown in Figure 5–33.
4. Choose a Distance of 4 px, 4 Steps, and Inset for the Direction. Click OK.
5. Repeat this for the other shadow we added next to the Photo. You may want to experiment with the settings in this dialog.

CHECKPOINT
This would be a good time to save your work. Choose File➔ Save As, and save this file in the directory of your choice as *stitch.fla*. Download the project at this point from
http://www.phptr.com/essential/flash5
or view it directly at
http://www.phptr.com/essential/flash5/stitch/stitch5-11.html.

You have now created the basic components of the splash screen. In the next chapter, you will add animation to this scene, create the main page with background animation, and create animated transitions for the main site.

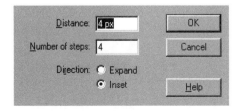

FIGURE 5–33 Soften Edges dialog.

RECAP

In this chapter, you've learned how to:

- Reshape an existing graphic
- Use intersections to create more complex shapes
- Use the Brush tool to create free form shapes

ADVANCED PROJECTS

1. In a new movie, create a rectangular shape with an unusual line style.
2. Change the fill with the Paint Bucket and the Line Style with the Ink Bottle.
3. Use the Arrow to add curves to the sides of the shape.
4. Create brush shapes with gradient fills.
5. Change the fills with the Paint Bucket and the Line Styles with the Ink Bottle.
6. Add and remove curves from the edges of the shapes, using the Arrow tool.

6 Advanced Animation

*T*he *Stitch Fashion Journal* site should present the site visitor with an eye-catching and memorable first impression. Like the Shelley page, it will have a splash screen, but it will be more dramatic than the Shelley animation. Not only will it be animated, but it will have background music as well.

◆ Animating Symbols

In the splash screen, one of the animated effects we will be creating is the rotating button image. The button needs to be made into a symbol and animated. We will be using a new animation technique to accomplish this. Thus far, you have used symbols as graphic objects for tweening; the animation resided in the main scene file. This isn't always practical to do. There will be times when you will want to duplicate a symbol and its animation, but not have to wade through a scene to capture the animation it does. Fortunately, Flash symbols can be self-animated. For example, if you wanted to animate the button spinning in the main scene, you would have to tediously rotate it slightly every few frames throughout the entire splash sequence. By self-animating the button, you will be able to create a much smaller sequence with a single rotation, and the button symbol will rotate throughout the splash sequence.

CHECKPOINT
Download the project at this point from
http://www.phptr.com/essential/flash5
or view it directly at
http://www.phptr.com/essential/flash5/stitch/stitch5-11.html.

Creating the Button Symbol

1. Select the Button layer.
2. When you click on a layer, everything in it is automatically selected. The button image should now be selected.
3. Choose Insert→Convert to Symbol.
4. Name it "Button" and choose Graphic for type. See Figure 6–1. Click OK.
5. Deselect the button image.
6. We should add the button shadow to the button symbol. Let's cut it from the main scene, keep it in memory, and add it to the button symbol. Start by selecting the button shadow. Be careful to get the entire shadow by clicking

FIGURE 6–1 Symbol Properties dialog box.

and dragging around it with the Arrow tool. When we soft-ened the edges in Chapter 5, a new outline was created. We want to make sure we get this as part of the symbol.

7. Choose Edit→Cut.
8. Select Edit→Edit Symbols.
9. Select the Button symbol from the symbol list to edit. Cre-ate a new layer and name it "Button Shadow."
10. Choose Edit→Paste and paste the shadow on the new layer.
11. Select and reposition the shadow as needed.
12. Name the original layer "Button Symbol."
13. Move the Button Shadow layer under the Button Symbol layer.

You should now have two layers for the button symbol in symbol editing mode. See Figure 6–2.

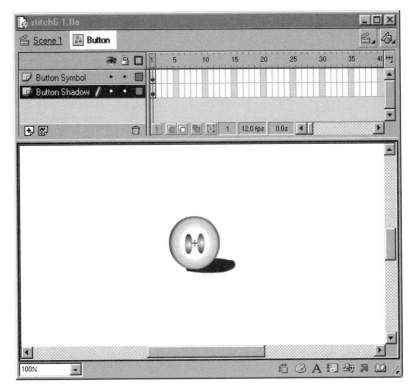

FIGURE 6–2 Button symbol with two layers.

CHECKPOINT

This would be a good time to save your work. Choose File→Save As, and save this file in the directory of your choice as *stitch.fla.* Download the project at this point from
http://www.phptr.com/essential/flash5
or view it directly at
http://www.phptr.com/essential/flash5/stitch/stitch6-1.html.

Animating the Button

Tweening is usually the easy way to create animations. In the case of the button, it's simpler just to do frame-by-frame animation, since we need just a few frames and we need to exercise tight control over them.

1. Begin by selecting the Button layer, and choose Edit→Edit Symbols. You should now be in symbol editing mode.
2. Hide the Button Shadow layer using the Layer menu.
3. Select the Button Symbol layer.
4. Choose Insert→Keyframe to add a new keyframe next to the current one, as shown in Figure 6–3. Select it.
5. Open the Transform panel, as shown in Figure 6–4.
6. Make sure the Rotate radio button is selected and enter 45 in the blank next to it. See Figure 6–5. Press Enter. The button is now rotated 45 degrees clockwise.
7. Insert another keyframe to the right of the current one. Select it.
8. Repeat steps 6 and 7 until the button has been rotated most of the way around. See Figure 6–6 for the progression. Here are the degrees to use: 0, 45, 90, 135, 180, –135, –90, –45.
9. You should now have eight keyframes for the button. Press the Enter key to view the animation.
10. Choose Show All from the Layers menu. The shadow appears only in the first frame. Let's fix that.
11. Select the Button Shadow layer. Click on the eighth frame and choose Insert→Frame. See Figure 6–7. The shadow will now appear in all the frames.

The button is now self-animated. It will appear to rotate throughout the main movie animation. It will loop automatically.

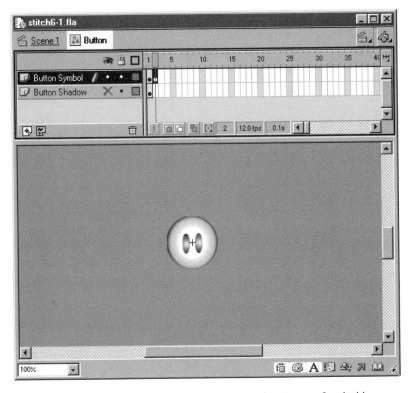

FIGURE 6–3 Button symbol with keyframe added to Button Symbol layer.

FIGURE 6–4
Rotate button.

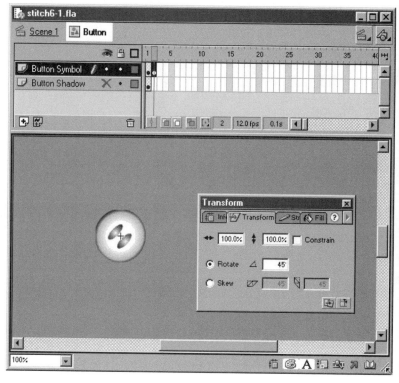

FIGURE 6–5 Rotate the button 45 degrees clockwise.

CHECKPOINT

This would be a good time to save your work. Choose File→Save As, and save this file in the directory of your choice as *stitch.fla*. Download the project at this point from
http://www.phptr.com/essential/flash5
or view it directly at
http://www.phptr.com/essential/flash5/stitch/stitch6-2.html.

FIGURE 6–6 Progression of the button rotation.

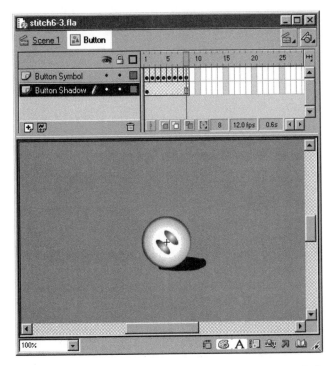

FIGURE 6–7 Button Shadow layer with eighth frame added.

Creating Other Symbols

A few other graphics on this page need to be turned into symbols so that we can animate them. This is a bit tedious, but it shouldn't take us very long.

1. To return to scene editing mode, choose Edit→Edit Movie.
2. If you have any hidden layers, choose Show All from the Layers menu.
3. Select the Fashion Journal text.
4. Choose Insert→Convert to Symbol. Name this "Fashion Text" and make it a Graphic. Click OK.
5. Select the photo.
6. Choose Insert→Convert to Symbol. Name this "Photo" and make it a Graphic. Click OK.
7. Select the Stitch text.

8. Choose Insert→Convert to Symbol. Name this "Stitch" and make it a Graphic. Click OK.

9. Select the needle.

10. Choose Insert→Convert to Symbol. Name this "Needle" and make it a Graphic. Click OK.

11. Select the shadow next to the photo. Be careful to get the entire shadow by clicking and dragging around it with the Arrow tool. When we softened the edges in Chapter 5, a new outline was created. We want to make sure we get this as part of the symbol.

12. Choose Insert→Convert to Symbol. Name this "Shadow" and make it a Graphic. Click OK.

13. Select the Blues text.

14. Choose Insert→Convert to Symbol. Name this "Blues" and make it a Graphic. Click OK.

15. Finally, select the thread. Choose Modify→Ungroup, but leave it selected.

16. Choose Insert→Convert to Symbol. Name this "Thread" and make it a Graphic. Click OK.

◆ Opening Sequence

The animation effects used for the opening sequence are somewhat more elaborate variations of what we used for the Shelley site. You will also be introduced to the motion layer.

Getting Started

The very first step for creating the splash screen is to decide how long you want the animation to be. We will make the *Stitch* splash screen last 135 frames, which at 12 fps is a little over 11 seconds.

1. Use the scroll bar just beneath the layers to scroll to layer 135. Click, hold, and drag the frame 135 of the first layer and drag down to select the frame 135 of all the layers. See Figure 6–8.

2. Choose Insert→Keyframe.

3. We will be working with the button image first, so select the Button layer, and choose Hide Others from the Layer menu.

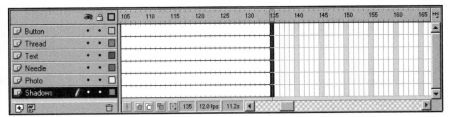

FIGURE 6-8 135th layer of all frames selected.

CHECKPOINT
This would be a good time to save your work. Choose File→Save As, and save this file in the directory of your choice as *stitch.fla*. Download the project at this point from
http://www.phptr.com/essential/flash5
or view it directly at
http://www.phptr.com/essential/flash5/stitch/stitch6-3.html.

Moving the Button Image

1. Insert a keyframe at frame 110 of the Button layer.
2. Select the first keyframe of the Button layer.
3. Make sure the Button symbol is selected and open the Info panel.
4. Change the X and Y settings in the Info panel to 50 and 100 respectively.
5. Change to the Transform panel and click in the Constrain box to make it checked. Type 500 in the width box. Notice that the height box also changes to 500. See Figure 6–9.

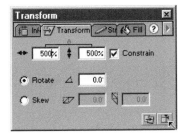

FIGURE 6–9
Transform panel.

FIGURE 6–10 View of the entire scene zoomed to 50%.

Press Enter. See Figure 6–10, which shows the entire scene, zoomed to 50%.

6. Insert a keyframe at frame 70 of the Button layer.
7. Click on the first keyframe again and open the Effect panel.
8. Select Alpha from the drop-down list and move the slider to zero, as shown in Figure 6–11.
9. Open the Frame panel.
10. Choose the Motion option for Tweening, set Scale checked, and Rotate set to Auto. See Figure 6–12. Click OK.
11. Click on the keyframe at 70. Choose the Motion option for Tweening type, set Scale checked, and Rotate set to Auto.

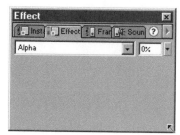

FIGURE 6–11
Effect panel.

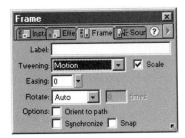

FIGURE 6–12
Frame panel.

CHECKPOINT
This would be a good time to save your work. Choose File→Save As, and save this file in the directory of your choice as *stitch.fla*. Download the project at this point from
http://www.phptr.com/essential/flash5
or view it directly at
http://www.phptr.com/essential/flash5/stitch/stitch6-4.html.

That is the complete button animation for the splash screen. Remember: If the location or size of the button isn't quite right at any point, it can be easily changed. Just click on the keyframe you wish to modify, select the button image with the Arrow, and use the Scale modifier to change it. To test the button animation, press Enter. Notice the rotation that we created in "Animating Symbols."

Fading in the Thread Image

The thread graphic will fade in, beginning at frame 90 and becoming completely visible at frame 110.

1. Select the Thread layer and hide the others.
2. Insert keyframes at frames 90 and 110.
3. Select the keyframe at frame 90. The thread symbol should be selected.
4. Open the Effect panel.
5. Select Alpha from the drop-down list and move the slider to zero
6. Repeat step 5 on the first keyframe. If you prefer, you can simply select and delete the graphic from the first keyframe.
7. Finally, click on the keyframe at frame 90, open the Frame panel, and set the Tweening to Motion.

CHECKPOINT

This would be a good time to save your work. Choose File→Save As, and save this file in the directory of your choice as *stitch.fla*. Download the project at this point from
http://www.phptr.com/essential/flash5
or view it directly at
http://www.phptr.com/essential/flash5/stitch/stitch6-5.html.

Stitch Text Animation and Fading

The Stitch title changes size, fades in and out, and moves around the scene. Instead of setting the tweening at the end of each step, this time you will add it all at once at the end.

1. Choose Show All from the Layers menu.
2. Insert a new layer and name it "Stitch."
3. Click on keyframe 1 of the Text layer.
4. Deselect everything and then select just the Stitch text and choose Edit→Cut.
5. Select the Stitch layer and hide the others.
6. Click on the first frame and choose Edit→Paste in Place.
7. Insert keyframes at frames 10, 20, 70, 95, and 135. See Figure 6–13.
8. Select the keyframe at frame 1 and make sure the Stitch title text is selected. Open the Transform panel and uncheck the Constrain box. Change the width to 120% and change the height to 550%, as shown in Figure 6–14. Open the Info panel and change X to 6 and Y to 92.
9. Figure 6–15 shows what the title should look like at the first keyframe.
10. Open the Effect panel.
11. Select Alpha from the drop-down list and move the slider to zero.

FIGURE 6–13 Stitch layer with keyframes inserted at frames 10, 20, 70, 95, and 135.

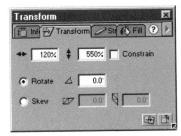

FIGURE 6–14
Transform panel.

12. Next, select the keyframe at frame 10 and make sure the Stitch title text is selected. Open the Transform panel and uncheck the Constrain box if it is checked. Change the width to 50% and change the height to 300%, as shown in Figure 6–16. Open the Info panel and change X to 350 and Y to 170.
13. The Stitch header should resemble Figure 6–17.
14. Select the keyframe at frame 20 and make sure the Stitch title text is selected. Open the Info panel and change X to 415 and Y to 215. This time, let's change the height and

FIGURE 6–15 Stitch title at first keyframe.

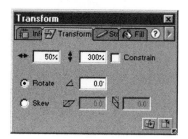

FIGURE 6–16
Transform panel.

width using the settings on the Info panel rather than the Transform panel. It is less exact, but it will accomplish what we need. Change width to 80 and height to 42, as shown in Figure 6–18.

15. The Stitch header should resemble Figure 6–19.
16. Open the Effect panel.
17. Select Alpha from the drop-down list and move the slider to zero.

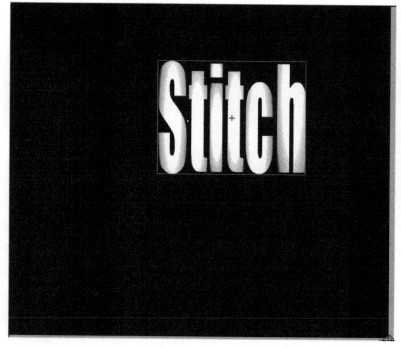

FIGURE 6–17 Stitch title at keyframe 10.

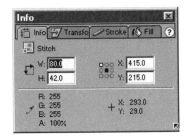

FIGURE 6–18
Info panel.

18. Select the keyframe at frame 70. Use the settings shown in the Info panel in Figure 6–20. These are a width of 292, height of 157, X of 42, and Y of 232.
19. The Stitch title should look like Figure 6–21.
20. Open the Effect panel.

FIGURE 6–19 Stitch title at keyframe 20.

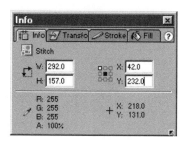

FIGURE 6–20
Info panel

21. Select Alpha from the drop-down list and move the slider to zero.
22. Finally, change the Tweening property for the keyframes at 1, 10, and 70 to Motion by clicking each one in turn and modifying the Frame panel.

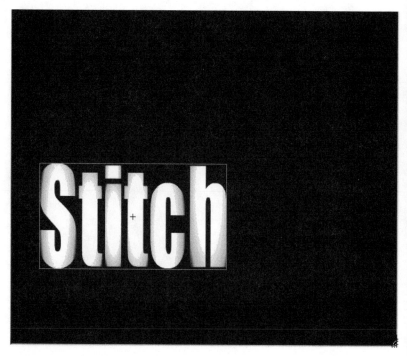

FIGURE 6–21 Stitch title at keyframe 70.

CHECKPOINT

This would be a good time to save your work. Choose File➔Save As, and save this file in the directory of your choice as *stitch.fla*. Download the project at this point from *http://www.phptr.com/essential/flash5* or view it directly at *http://www.phptr.com/essential/flash5/stitch/stitch6-6.html.*

Fashion Text Animation and Fading

The text Fashion Journal behaves in almost the same way as the Stitch title.

1. Choose Show All from the Layers menu.
2. Insert a new layer and name it "Fashion."
3. Click on keyframe 1 of the Text layer.
4. Select the Fashion Journal text and choose Edit➔Cut.
5. Select the Fashion layer and hide the others.
6. Click on the first keyframe and choose Edit➔Paste in Place.
7. Insert keyframes at frames 20, 30, 40, 70, 110, and 135.
8. Select the keyframe at frame 1 and delete the Fashion Journal image by selecting it and pressing the Delete key.
9. Select the keyframe at frame 20 and use the Info panel to change the Fashion Journal image to the settings in Figure 6–22. These are a width of 592, height of 298, X of 4, and Y of 114.
10. The image should look like Figure 6–23.
11. Open the Effect panel.
12. Select Alpha from the drop-down list and move the slider to zero.

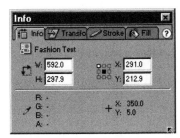

FIGURE 6–22
Info panel.

FIGURE 6–23 Fashion Journal text at keyframe 20.

13. Select the keyframe at frame 40 and use Info panel to change the Fashion Journal image to the settings in Figure 6–24. These are a width of 92, height of 18, X of 396, and Y of 244.

14. The Fashion Journal graphic should look like Figure 6–25.

15. Open the Effect panel.

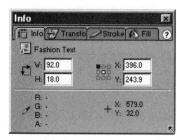

FIGURE 6–24
Info panel.

FIGURE 6–25 Fashion Journal text at keyframe 40.

16. Select Alpha from the drop-down list and move the slider to zero.
17. Select the keyframe at frame 70 and use the Info panel to change the Fashion Journal image to the settings in Figure 6–26. These are a width of 312, height of 60, X of 5, and Y of 15.

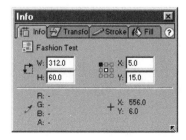

FIGURE 6–26
Info panel.

FIGURE 6–27 Fashion Journal text at keyframe 70.

18. The Fashion Journal graphic should look like Figure 6–27.
19. Open the Effect panel.
20. Select Alpha from the drop-down list and move the slider to zero.
21. Finally, change the Tweening property for the keyframes at 20, 30, and 70 to Motion by clicking each one in turn and modifying the Frame panel.

CHECKPOINT
This would be a good time to save your work. Choose File→Save As, and save this file in the directory of your choice as *stitch.fla*. Download the project at this point from
http://www.phptr.com/essential/flash5
or view it directly at
http://www.phptr.com/essential/flash5/stitch/stitch6-7.html.

Blues Text with Motion Layer

The Blues text will use a new technique, known as a Motion Guide, to specify its motion.

1. Choose Show All Layers from the Layers menu.
2. Rename the Text layer to Blues.
3. Select the Blues layer. Hide the other layers.
4. Select the keyframe at 135 and use Edit→Clear on the Stitch and Fashion Journal images so that only the Blues text remains.
5. Insert a keyframe at frame 110.
6. Select the Blues graphic at keyframe 1 and choose Edit→Clear.
7. Select the keyframe at 110, and use the Info panel to move the Blues text to the location shown in Figure 6–28, an X of 275 and Y of 414.
8. The scene should look like Figure 6–29.
9. Choose the Layer menu option Add Motion Guide. A new layer appears above the current Blues layer. Select this new layer.
10. Insert a keyframe into this new layer at 110. Select the keyframe at 110.
11. Change to the Line Tool with the Stroke panel size set to 1.0, the color white, and the style Solid. See Figure 6–30.
12. Draw a small line from the center of the text up and to the right, as shown in Figure 6–31.
13. Use the Arrow tool to move the ends of this line as needed. The top should be near the center of the Blues text at frame 135. The bottom should be at the center of the Blues text at frame 110. See Figure 6–32. Be extra careful here to line up the ends to the center. This can be a little

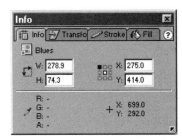

FIGURE 6–28
Info panel.

FIGURE 6–29 Blues text at keyframe 110.

tricky. Choosing View→Snap to Objects will help you line it up. Make sure you turn Snap to Objects back off after you are done with it.

14. Using the Arrow tool, click and hold near the middle of the line and drag to the left, as shown in Figure 6–33.
15. Select keyframe 110 of the Blues layer.
16. Open the Effect panel. Select Alpha from the drop-down list and move the slider to zero.

FIGURE 6–30
Stroke panel.

FIGURE 6–31 Line drawn from the center of text up and to the right.

FIGURE 6–32 Blues text at frame 135.

FIGURE 6–33 Curve added to line.

17. The final step is to add motion tweening to keyframe 110 of the Blues layer. The text should now follow that path. The path you created will not show up in the .swf movie when you publish it. You may wish to hide the motion layer using the Layer menu.

CHECKPOINT

This would be a good time to save your work. Choose File→Save As, and save this file in the directory of your choice as *stitch.fla*. Download the project at this point from
http://www.phptr.com/essential/flash5
or view it directly at
http://www.phptr.com/essential/flash5/stitch/stitch6-8.html.

Needle Rotation, Fading, and Movement

The needle graphic fades in rapidly while rotating and moving.

1. Select the Needle layer and hide others.
2. Insert keyframes at 70 and 95.
3. Select keyframe 1 and use Edit→Clear to delete the needle image.
4. Select keyframe 70. Use the Arrow tool with the Resize and Rotate buttons to make the needle look like Figure 6–34.

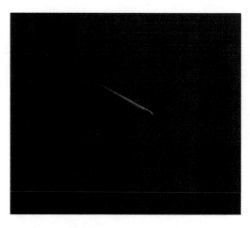

FIGURE 6–34 Needle appearance at keyframe 70.

5. The head of the needle is pointed toward the bottom right corner of the scene.
6. Open the Effect panel.
7. Select Alpha from the drop-down list and move the slider to zero.
8. Set motion tweening on frame 70 using the Frame panel.

CHECKPOINT

This would be a good time to save your work. Choose File→Save As, and save this file in the directory of your choice as *stitch.fla*. Download the project at this point from
http://www.phptr.com/essential/flash5
or view it directly at
http://www.phptr.com/essential/flash5/stitch/stitch6-9.html.

Text Shadow Movement, Shape, and Tint

1. Select the Shadows layer and hide the others.
2. Insert a keyframe at 110 and select it.
3. Change the shape to resemble Figure 6–35. You will need to use the Rotate and Scale settings on the Arrow tool. To make it a bit more visible while editing it, you may need to temporarily change the movie background color by

FIGURE 6–35
Shadow shape at keyframe 110.

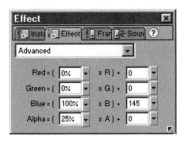

FIGURE 6–36
Effect panel.

selecting Modify→Movie. A light color will make the shadow more visible.

4. If you changed the movie background, change it back to the original dark blue color.
5. Click on the graphic at keyframe 70 and open the Effect panel.
6. Choose Advanced from the drop-down list. The Advanced option allows you to combine both transparency and color hue effects at the same time.
7. Use the settings shown in Figure 6–36. These are 0% for Red, 0% for Green, 100% for Blue, and 25% for Alpha. Use an RGB of 0, 0, 145 and 0 for A.
8. Add motion tweening to keyframe 110 of this layer.
9. The final step is to select the first keyframe and Edit→Clear the Shadow graphic.

CHECKPOINT
This would be a good time to save your work. Choose File→Save As, and save this file in the directory of your choice as *stitch.fla*. Download the project at this point from
http://www.phptr.com/essential/flash5
or view it directly at
http://www.phptr.com/essential/flash5/stitch/stitch6-10.html.

Photograph Fade-in

1. Select the Photo layer and hide others.
2. Insert keyframes at 95 and 110.
3. Select frame 95.

4. Open the Effect panel.
5. Select Alpha from the drop-down list and move the slider to zero.
6. Add motion tweening to keyframe 95 of this layer.
7. Select the first keyframe and delete the Photo image.

CHECKPOINT

This would be a good time to save your work. Choose File→Save As, and save this file in the directory of your choice as *stitch.fla*. Download the project at this point from
http://www.phptr.com/essential/flash5
or view it directly at
http://www.phptr.com/essential/flash5/stitch/stitch6-11.html.

We should drag the layers into their proper order. The final order of the layers, from top to bottom, is:
- Button
- Fashion
- Stitch
- Thread
- Guide: Blues
- Blues
- Needle
- Shadows
- Photo

You have now finished the splash screen animation. Time to add some background music!

◆ Background Music

You will be creating a new movie that will be called by our *Stitch* splash movie. The movie will consist of a WAV or AIFF file and a switch to turn the music on and off.

Creating the New Movie

1. Choose File→New.
2. Uncheck View→Work Area if it's checked.

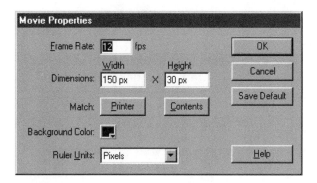

FIGURE 6–37 Movie Properties settings for new movie.

3. Select Modify→Movie.
4. Change the movie size to 150 px by 30 px. Change the background to the same dark blue as you used in the main movie. See Figure 6–37.
5. Decide on which WAV, AIFF, or mp3 file you wish to use. The one used in the example is *stitch.wav* and is available as a WAV and AIFF file at *http://www.phptr.com/essential/ flash5/stitch/music/*. Smaller file size is definitely preferable.
6. Choose File→Import and locate the file you wish to use.
7. Save this movie as *music.fla* in the same directory as your splash screen.

CHECKPOINT
This would be a good time to save your work. Choose File→Save As, and save this file in the directory of your choice as *stitch.fla*. Download the project at this point from
http://www.phptr.com/essential/flash5
or view it directly at
http://www.phptr.com/essential/flash5/stitch/music6-1.html.

Creating the First Button

1. Make sure View→Antialias Text is checked.
2. Choose Window→Library.

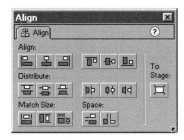

FIGURE 6-38
Align panel.

3. Click on the Options menu on the right top of this dialog box and choose New Symbol.
4. Name this symbol "Turn Off" and make it a button. Click OK.
5. You are now presented with the symbol editing interface.
6. Using the Text tool, type the words "turn off music" with the font Impact or the font of your choice. Use a font size of 20, and white for the color.
7. Select this graphic. Open the Align panel.
8. Use the settings shown in Figure 6–38 to center the image.
9. Click under the Over frame label and insert a keyframe. See Figure 6–39.
10. Change to the Text tool. Highlight the words. Use the Character panel to change the color to a medium gray.

CHECKPOINT
This would be a good time to save your work. Choose File→Save As, and save this file in the directory of your choice as *stitch.fla*. Download the project at this point from
http://www.phptr.com/essential/flash5
or view it directly at
http://www.phptr.com/essential/flash5/stitch/music6-2.html.

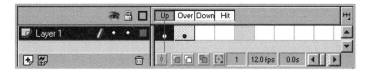

FIGURE 6-39 Keyframe inserted for Over frame.

Creating the Second Button

Creating the second button is very simple.

1. If the Library isn't open, choose Window→Library.
2. Click on the Turn Off button in the Library.
3. Click on the Options button on the top right of the Library dialog box and choose Duplicate.
4. Name this new button "Turn On." Double-click on this new button to edit it. You should now be in editing mode for the Turn On button.
5. Change to the Text tool and change the text to read "turn on music." You will need to do this for both the Up and Over keyframes.

CHECKPOINT

This would be a good time to save your work. Choose File→Save As, and save this file in the directory of your choice as *stitch.fla*. Download the project at this point from
http://www.phptr.com/essential/flash5
or view it directly at
http://www.phptr.com/essential/flash5/stitch/music6-3.html.

Creating the Movie Clip

The sound needs to be embedded with the buttons in a movie clip.

1. If the Library isn't open, choose Window→Library.
2. Click on the Options menu on the right top of this dialog box and choose New Symbol.
3. Name this symbol "Toggle" and make it a movie clip. Click OK.
4. You are now in symbol editing mode for the Toggle movie clip. Add two new layers. See Figure 6–40. You should now have three. Name them "Action," "Button," and "Music."

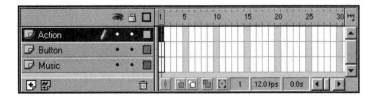

FIGURE 6–40 Movie with Action, Button, and Music layers.

CHECKPOINT
This would be a good time to save your work. Choose File→Save As, and save this file in the directory of your choice as *stitch.fla*. Download the project at this point from
http://www.phptr.com/essential/flash5
or view it directly at
http://www.phptr.com/essential/flash5/stitch/music6-4.html.

Inserting the Buttons in the Movie

1. Select the Button layer.
2. Insert a keyframe at frame 10. Select the frame located at frame 1.
3. In the Library dialog box, click on the Turn Off button you created.
4. Click, hold, and drag the image from the Library to the work area.
5. Center the image using the Align panel. You may have to use the scroll bars on the side of the work area to see the center of the window.
6. Select the keyframe located at frame 10.
7. In the Library dialog box, click on the Turn On button you created.
8. Click, hold, and drag the image from the Library to the Scene.
9. Center the image using the Align panel.

CHECKPOINT

This would be a good time to save your work. Choose File➔Save As, and save this file in the directory of your choice as *stitch.fla*. Download the project at this point from
http://www.phptr.com/essential/flash5
or view it directly at
http://www.phptr.com/essential/flash5/stitch/music6-5.html.

Modifying the Action Layer

1. Click on the Action layer of the Toggle button.
2. Select frame 1 of this layer. Open the Frame panel.
3. Enter "off" for the Label.
4. Double-click on frame 1 to open the Frame Actions dialog. Double-click on Stop under Basic Actions. Close the Frame Actions dialog.
5. Insert a keyframe at frame 10 of the Action layer.
6. Select this new keyframe. Open the Frame panel.
7. Enter "on" for the Label.
8. Double-click on this frame to open the Frame Actions dialog. Double-click on Stop under Basic Actions. Close the Frame Actions dialog. See Figure 6–41.
9. Select the keyframe at frame 1 of the Button layer.
10. Using the Arrow, select the Turn Off Music graphic. Right-click (PC) or Ctrl-click (Mac) and choose Actions. This opens the Object Actions dialog.
11. Double-click on On MouseEvent under Basic Actions.
12. Check Press from the Parameters on the bottom. See Figure 6–42.
13. Now double-click on Go To.
14. Change the Type setting on the bottom to Frame Label and choose "on" from the drop-down list next to Frame. See Figure 6–43. Uncheck "Go To and Play." Close the dialog.
15. We need to add actions to the other button also. Select the keyframe at frame 10 of the Button layer.
16. Using the Arrow, select the Turn On Music graphic. Right-click (PC) or Ctrl-click (Mac) and choose Actions. This opens the Object Actions dialog.

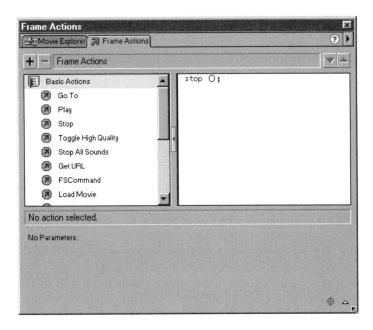

FIGURE 6–41 Actions tab with Stop action added.

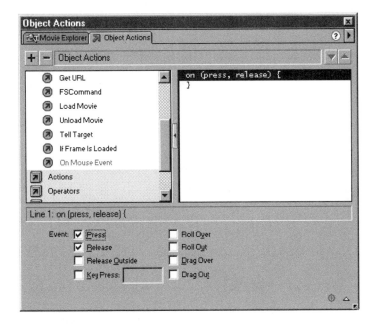

FIGURE 6–42 Actions tab with On Press event added.

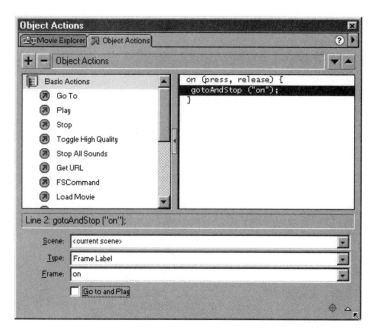

FIGURE 6–43 Actions tab with Go To and Stop event added.

17. Double-click on On MouseEvent under Basic Actions.
18. Check Press from the Parameters on the bottom.
19. Now double-click on Go To. Uncheck "Go To and Play."
20. Change the Type setting on the bottom to Frame Label and choose "off" from the drop-down list next to Frame. Close the dialog.

CHECKPOINT

This would be a good time to save your work. Choose File→Save As, and save this file in the directory of your choice as *stitch.fla*. Download the project at this point from
http://www.phptr.com/essential/flash5
or view it directly at
http://www.phptr.com/essential/flash5/stitch/music6-6.html.

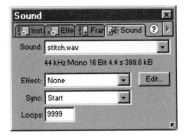

FIGURE 6–44
Sound tab with *stitch.wav* selected.

Adding Music to the Music Layer

1. Click on the Music layer.
2. Click on the frame at frame 1.
3. Open the Sound panel.
4. Choose *stitch.wav* or *stitch.aiff* from the Sound drop-down list.
5. Set Effect to None, Sync to Start, and Loops to 9999. See Figure 6–44.
6. Insert a keyframe at frame 10 of the Music layer.
7. Click on the new keyframe at frame 10.
8. Return to the Sound panel.
9. Choose *stitch.wav* or *stitch.aiff* from the Sound drop-down list.
10. Set Effect to None, Sync to Stop, and Loops to 0. See Figure 6–45.

The Toggle button is now complete. To add it to the main music movie, choose Edit→Edit Movie and drag the Toggle movie clip from the library to the stage. You can test it by selecting Control→Test Movie.

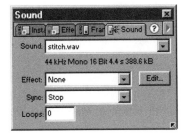

FIGURE 6–45
Sound panel.

CHECKPOINT

This would be a good time to save your work. Choose File→Save As, and save this file in the directory of your choice as *stitch.fla*. Download the project at this point from
http://www.phptr.com/essential/flash5
or view it directly at
http://www.phptr.com/essential/flash5/stitch/music6-7.html.

Adding the Clip to the Splash Screen

We have one last task in front of us, and that is to add the Toggle movie clip to our *Stitch* splash movie.

1. Open the *stitch6-11.fla* file. This may also be downloaded from *http://www.phptr.com/essential/flash5/stitch/stitch6-11.fla.*
2. Create a new layer in the *Stitch* movie and call it "Music." Click on the first frame in this layer.
3. Choose File→Open as Library and choose the finished *music.fla* file. This opens the Library for the music movie.
4. Drag the Toggle movie clip into the upper left corner of the *Stitch* movie. See Figure 6–46. You may want to resize it with the Arrow Tool and the Scale option selected.

CHECKPOINT

This would be a good time to save your work. Choose File→Save As, and save this file in the directory of your choice as *stitch.fla*. Download the project at this point from
http://www.phptr.com/essential/flash5
or view it directly at
http://www.phptr.com/essential/flash5/stitch/stitch6-12.html.

Test the movie by selecting Control→Test Movie.

Now that the splash screen is completed, we will move on to creating more advanced menuing systems and frame actions, a form, and an interactive fashion show.

turn off music

FIGURE 6–46 Toggle movie clip.

RECAP

In this chapter you've learned how to:
- Animate symbols
- Create an opening sequence
- Add background music and a button to control it

ADVANCED PROJECTS

1. Make a copy of the current movie file and change the animation.
2. Modify the motion path of the Blues shadow.
3. Change the music used in the splash screen.
4. Create your own movie and add the music movie to it.

7 Advanced Effects

Until now, you have created straightforward animation with no fancy frame actions. In this chapter, you will be shown how to create animated buttons, make a transition from one scene to another, open movies in other browser windows, and stop an animation. You will also be creating a simple comment form, changing the mouse cursor, and putting together an interactive movie.

◆ Animated Buttons

In this section you will create a button that will be reused throughout the *Stitch* site and in the interactive activity. Instead of having a static graphic for the Over state, the button will play a movie clip.

CHECKPOINT
Download the project at this point from
http://www.phptr.com/essential/flash5
or view it directly at
http://www.phptr.com/essential/flash5/stitch/stitch6-12.html.

Creating the Parent Button

1. Begin by opening the current *stitch.fla* file.
2. Select Window→Library to open the symbol library for this file.
3. In the Library dialog box, click the Options button and choose New Symbol.
4. Name this "Parent" and choose type Button. You are presented with the symbol editing screen for your new symbol. It is currently blank.
5. In the Library window, locate the Button symbol. Select it and choose Edit from the Options menu. You will be using this graphic as part of the new Parent button.
6. Select the Button Symbol layer and choose Hide Others from the Layer menu. See Figure 7–1.
7. Select the button image in frame 1 and choose Edit→Copy.
8. Use the Symbol List button on the top right of the scene to change to the Parent symbol.
9. Click on the Up keyframe and choose Edit→Paste in Place.
10. Open the Info panel.
11. Select the button image in the Up keyframe. Change its location and size to the values shown in Figure 7–2. These are a width of 50, height of 50, X of –25, and Y of –25.
12. Add keyframes for Over and Down.
13. Click on the Down keyframe. Select the button image with the Arrow. Change Info panel values to those shown in Figure 7–3. These are a width of 40, height of 40, X of –20, and Y of –20.

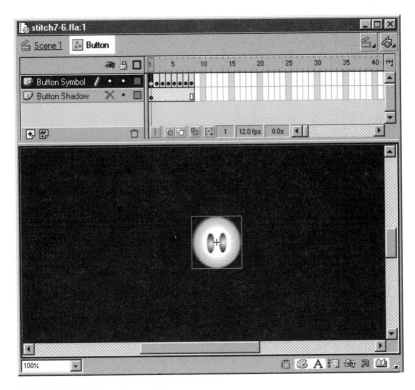

FIGURE 7–1 Button Symbol layer.

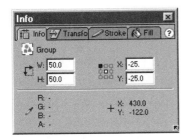

FIGURE 7–2
Info panel.

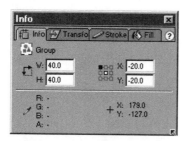

FIGURE 7–3
Info panel.

Creating the Movie Clip

Now that the button has been created, you still need to create the movie clip to add to it.

1. Highlight the Button symbol in the Library dialog box.
2. Choose Duplicate from the Options menu.
3. Name the new symbol "Rotation" and make it a movie clip.
4. Use the Symbol List button to change to the Rotation symbol.
5. We will not be using the button shadow in this movie. Delete the Button Shadow layer on this new symbol by selecting it and choosing Delete Layer from the Layer menu. Make certain you are deleting the Button Shadow layer, not the Button symbol itself, from the Rotation symbol.

Adding the Movie Clip to the Button Over State

1. Return to the Parent symbol. Select the Over keyframe.
2. Drag the Rotation movie clip you just created from the Library window onto the work area. You will now have two button images showing.
3. Delete the old one.
4. Select the remaining image. Change its location and size to the values shown in Figure 7–2. These are a width of 50, height of 50, X of –25, and Y of –25.

That's it! You have now created an animated button. If you want to test it, open a new blank document and drag the Parent button in it. Then choose Control→Test Movie and check out the mouse states.

In the next section, you will create the main menu scene and a transition to it from the splash animation.

CHECKPOINT
This would be a good time to save your work. Choose File→Save As, and save this file in the directory of your choice as *shelley.fla*. Download the project at this point from
http://www.phptr.com/essential/flash5
or view it directly at
http://www.phptr.com/essential/flash5/stitch/stitch7-1.html.

◆ Transitions

Before you can create a transition from one scene to the next, you need to create a second scene.

Creating a New Scene

1. Begin by opening the current *stitch.fla* file if necessary.
2. If you need to do it, choose Edit→Edit Movie to leave Symbol Editing mode.
3. Next, choose Window→Panels→Scene.
4. Click on the Add Scene button on the Scene panel, shown in Figure 7–4.
5. Double-click on the name of this new scene, Scene 2. See Figure 7–5. Name this new scene "Menu."
6. Since this scene has a name, you should give the original scene a name also. Double-click Scene 1 and name this scene "Splash."

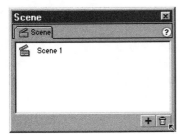

FIGURE 7–4
Scene panel.

The Menu scene you will end up with is shown in Figure 7–6. The transition will consist of most of the graphics fading out. The button will roll across the page and then down, leaving a trail of links behind it. The needle will grow larger and move left, and the thread will lengthen.

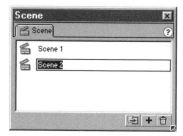

FIGURE 7–5
Scene panel.

FIGURE 7–6 Menu scene.

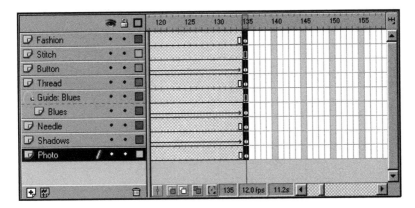

FIGURE 7–7 Last frame of all layers selected at the same time.

Copying Frames

To do a successful transition from one scene to the next, you need to start the new scene where the old one stopped. So you will be copying the last frame of all the layers of the Splash scene to the first frame of the Menu scene. This sounds more confusing than it is.

1. Make sure the scene currently showing is Splash. You can change scenes with the Scene List button on the top right of the movie window.
2. Press and hold the Ctrl key. At the same time, click and hold on the last frame on the top layer. If you are on a Mac, you may need to use the Shift key.
3. Drag straight down with the mouse to select the last frame for all the layers at the same time. See Figure 7–7.
4. Choose Edit→Copy Frames.
5. Change to the Menu scene. Click on the first frame of Layer 1.
6. Choose Edit→Paste Frames. The Menu scene now looks just like the last frame of the Splash scene. Make sure that the layer names came over as well. If you need to, flip back and forth between the scenes and change your layer names back to the originals from the Splash scene.

7. Let's remove the music from the Menu scene. Just click on the Music layer and choose Delete Layer from the Layer menu.

8. Finally, we don't need the Blues Text motion guide anymore, so delete this layer also.

CHECKPOINT

This would be a good time to save your work. Choose File→Save As, and save this file in the directory of your choice as *shelley.fla*. Download the project at this point from
http://www.phptr.com/essential/flash5
or view it directly at
http://www.phptr.com/essential/flash5/stitch/stitch7-2.html.

Fading Out Images

It's time to add the animation for the transition. The first part of the transition consists of most of the images fading out.

1. Select the tenth frame of all the layers and choose Insert Keyframe.

2. Click on the tenth frame of the Fashion layer. If you are not sure which image you are dealing with, you can select Hide Others from the layer menu.

3. Click on the Fashion Journal text and open the Effect panel.

4. Select Alpha from the drop down list, as shown in Figure 7–8, and set the slider to 0%.

5. Repeat steps 4 and 5 for the following layers: Blues, Shadows, and Photo. Make sure you have the tenth frame selected when you make the Alpha changes.

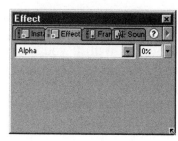

FIGURE 7–8
Color Effect tab.

CHECKPOINT

This would be a good time to save your work. Choose File➔Save As, and save this file in the directory of your choice as *shelley.fla.* Download the project at this point from
http://www.phptr.com/essential/flash5
or view it directly at
http://www.phptr.com/essential/flash5/stitch/stitch7-3.html.

Moving and Resizing the Other Images

The images that are still visible at keyframe 10 are the Stitch header, the button, the needle, and the thread. These will all be used as part of the transition animation. Take a look at Figure 7–9 to preview the positions and sizes to which we will be moving these graphics at the tenth frame.

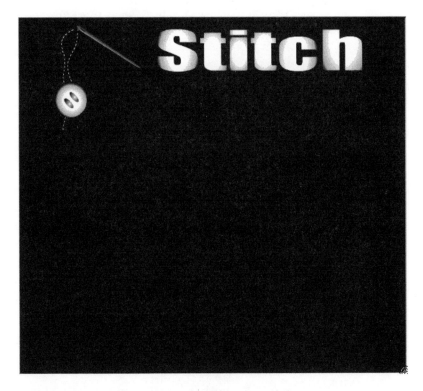

FIGURE 7–9 Positions and sizes of graphics at tenth frame.

1. First, click on the Stitch layer keyframe at frame 10.
2. Open the Info panel. Change the values for the Stitch header, as shown in Figure 7–10. These are a width of 320, height of 60, X of 215, and Y of 15.
3. Select the needle. To move it up and to the left and make it quite a bit smaller, use the settings in Figure 7–11. These are a width of 100, height of 60, X of 90, and Y of 10.
4. Move the thread so it seems to be attached to the eye of the needle.
5. Rotate the thread so it is hanging down, and resize it to resemble Figure 7–12. You may have to move it after rotation to put it back in the needle eye.
6. Use the Info panel shown in Figure 7–13 to move the button underneath the needle and make it slightly smaller. These are a width of 65, height of 52, X of 55, and Y of 90.
7. Finally, select all frames for all layers by holding the Ctrl key and clicking and holding on the top layer and dragging downward and to the right. If you are using a Mac, you may have to use Select Open the Frame panel and select Motion from the Tweening drop-down box, as shown in Figure 7–14.

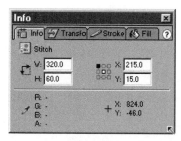

FIGURE 7–10
Info panel.

FIGURE 7–11
Info panel.

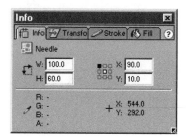

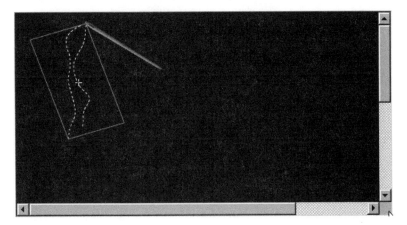

FIGURE 7–12 Thread rotated to hang down.

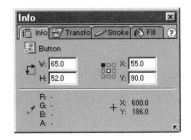

FIGURE 7–13
Info panel.

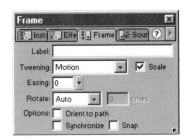

FIGURE 7–14
Frame panel.

CHECKPOINT

This would be a good time to save your work. Choose File→Save As, and save this file in the directory of your choice as *shelley.fla*. Download the project at this point from
http://www.phptr.com/essential/flash5
or view it directly at
http://www.phptr.com/essential/flash5/stitch/stitch7-4.html.

Adding More Motion to the Button Symbol

In the transition animation, the Button symbol moves straight down, leaving behind the link buttons.

1. Select the Button layer. You may want to hide the other layers.
2. Add a keyframe at frame 45.
3. Choose View→Work Area and make sure it's checked.
4. Choose View→Magnification and set it to 50%.
5. Select View→Grid→Show Grid and View→Grid→Snap to Grid.
6. Select the new keyframe at 45. Hold down the Shift key and select and move the button straight down until it is off the screen. Holding down Shift helps you drag it in a straight line.

Putting in the Link Buttons

The link buttons on this page appear to come from behind the large button as it moves downward.

1. Create a new layer and name it "Links."
2. Drag the new layer to the top of the list. You will be moving it back down after you are done.
3. Use the Layer menu to hide all the layers except for the Links layer.
4. Click on the red X next to the Button layer to make it visible also.
5. Select the Links layer and create a keyframe at 10. Select it.
6. Select the Text Tool. Open the Character panel and select a light blue color. Select Impact, or the font of your choice, and a font size of 48.

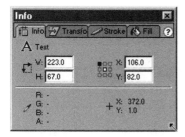

FIGURE 7–15
Info panel.

7. Type the words "Blues Issue."
8. Select this text and use the Info panel settings shown in Figure 7–15 to resize and move the Blues Issue text. These are a width of 223, height of 67, X of 106, and Y of 82.
9. Add a keyframe to the Links layer at frame 15. Select it.
10. Open the Window→Library and select the Parent button from the list.
11. Drag the image from the Library to the scene and place it on top of the larger button, as shown in Figure 7–16.
12. Insert a keyframe at frame 20 of the Links layer and drag another Parent button on the scene, as shown in Figure 7–17.

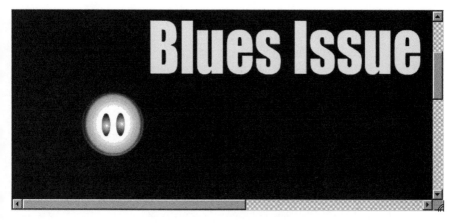

FIGURE 7–16 Button placed on top of larger button at frame 15.

FIGURE 7–17 Button placed on top of larger button at frame 20.

13. Repeat step 12 at frame 25 and then frame 30. Keyframe 30 should look like Figure 7–18.
14. Insert a final keyframe at 45.
15. The Blues Issue text will be animated to come out from behind the button and will grow when we reorganize the layers. Select the Links keyframe at frame 10.
16. Select the Blues Issue text. Open the Info panel and use the settings shown in Figure 7–19. This will resize and move the text so that it is completely on top of the button. These are a width of 35, height of 34, X of 66, and Y of 105.
17. Open the Frame panel and click keyframe 10. Set the Tweening to Motion.
18. Finally, drag the Links layer down to the bottom of the layer list. One important thing: Make sure the only keyframe in this layer with tweening set is 10. The rest should all have tweening set to none.

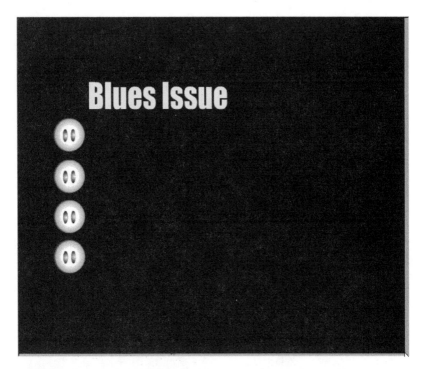

FIGURE 7–18 All four buttons placed.

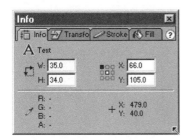

FIGURE 7–19
Info panel.

CHECKPOINT
This would be a good time to save your work. Choose File→Save As, and save this file in the directory of your choice as *shelley.fla*. Download the project at this point from
http://www.phptr.com/essential/flash5
or view it directly at
http://www.phptr.com/essential/flash5/stitch/stitch7-5.html.

Adding the Articles and Photos

The article text and photos are static. They are in their own layer and simply appear at frame 15.

1. Insert and select a new layer, called "Articles."
2. Choose Hide Others from the Layer menu.
3. Click on the red X next to the Links layer to make it visible also.
4. Insert a keyframe at frame 15 of the Articles layer.
5. Select the keyframe at 15 of the Articles layer.
6. Change to the Text tool. Open the Character panel. Use Impact or the font of your choice, font color white. Enter a font size of 26 in the font size box.
7. Enter the article names, as shown in Figure 7–20. Don't worry about their locations; we will move them shortly.
8. Select the frame at 30 and move the article names next to the buttons, as shown in Figure 7–21. The article names

FIGURE 7–20 Article names.

FIGURE 7–21 Article names moved next to buttons.

are "Vacation Blues," "Evening Blues," "Blue Monday,"
and "Moody Blues." Don't move the buttons, just the article text. Feel free to use the Align panel, Grid and Snap to
Grid, and to increase the zoom amount to assist in lining
up the links.

9. You will need to get the photos from the Web site to
   import. They can be downloaded from *http://
   www.phptr.com/essential/flash5/stitch/misc/photos.html.*

10. Select keyframe 15 of the Articles layer again. Choose
    File→Import to select the four photos and place them on
    the page, as shown in Figure 7–22. You can hold down the
    Ctrl key and select all four at once from the Import dialog
    in Windows. On a Mac, you may have to select these one
    at a time.

11. The imported images can be resized with the Arrow tool,
    using the Scale option. They can be reordered using the
    Modify→Arrange options.

FIGURE 7–22 Four photos placed on scene.

CHECKPOINT

This would be a good time to save your work. Choose File→Save As, and save this file in the directory of your choice as *shelley.fla*. Download the project at this point from
http://www.phptr.com/essential/flash5
or view it directly at
http://www.phptr.com/essential/flash5/stitch/stitch7-6.html.

Lengthening the Thread

You have only one last animation step, stretching out the thread.

1. Choose Show All from the Layer menu.
2. Insert a keyframe at 45 for any layers that do not have one.
3. Select keyframe 45 of the Thread layer. Click on the thread graphic with the Arrow. Turn on the Scale option.

4. Drag the thread downward until it is long enough to reach the bottom of the page. You will have to move the thread to line up with the eye of the needle again. Refer to Figure 7–6 for a better idea of what it should look like.

5. You won't have to add motion tweening, because it is already present. When you added the keyframe at frame 45, keyframe 10 had tweening set and anything in between 10 and 45 is tweened by default.

Now that you have two scenes, your movie will display the splash scene animation, followed by the second, but then it will display the first scene again and continue looping. It is very important that you tell the Flash player to stop at the end of the Menu scene.

Stopping the Action at the End of the Menu Scene Animation

Here's how to set a stop action at the end of the Menu scene.

1. Choose any one of the keyframes at 45. It does not matter which layer you choose. The example site uses the Button layer.

2. Double-click on this frame to open the Frame Actions dialog.

3. From the Basic Actions menu, double-click on Stop, as shown in Figure 7–23. Close the dialog. Now the player will stop at that frame.

CHECKPOINT

This would be a good time to save your work. Choose File→Save As, and save this file in the directory of your choice as *shelley.fla*. Download the project at this point from
http://www.phptr.com/essential/flash5
or directly
http://www.phptr.com/essential/flash5/stitch/stitch7-7.html.

Since you have already learned how to call other pages with button actions in Chapter 3, we won't cover that in detail here. Remember: To add a link to a button, simply set its Action to Get

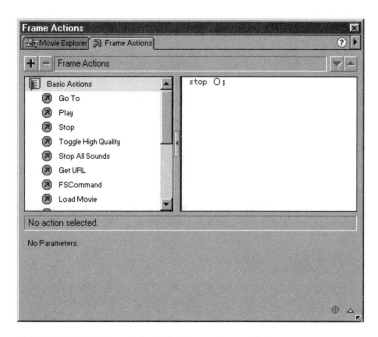

FIGURE 7–23 Actions tab with Stop action added.

URL and specify a page on the right. In this case, you should double-click each of the buttons in keyframe 45 to access its Instance Property dialog box and use that Actions tab.

Now that the drudge work of creating a menu page is out of the way, it's time to create a simple comment form with Flash.

◆ Forms

This section will show you how to create an extremely simple Flash 4 form for soliciting comments from visitors to the *Stitch* site. The form consists of two text fields, a subject box and comments box. When the Submit button is clicked, the form is emailed to an email address embedded in the button action. Although the form presented here doesn't interact with a CGI script, it can easily be modified to do so.

Creating the Form

The comment form is very simple, consisting of a title, two text fields with labels, and an OK button. Figure 7–24 shows you what the form will look like.

1. You'll need to create a new movie. Choose File→New.
2. Choose Modify→Movie. Change the movie size to 600 pixels by 500 pixels.
3. Change the background color to the same dark blue used for the *Stitch* site. Click OK.
4. Change to the Rectangle tool, shown in Figure 7–25. Set the line color to be transparent, and the fill to a medium gray.
5. Draw a small rectangle.
6. Open the Info panel.
7. Use the Arrow to select the rectangle you just created.
8. Change the location and size to the settings shown in Figure 7–26. These are a width of 388, height of 362, X of 95, and Y of 96.

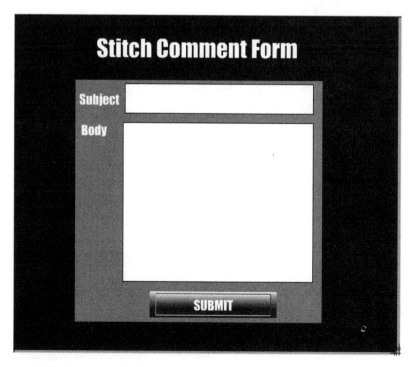

FIGURE 7–24 Stitch Comment Form.

FIGURE 7–25
Rectangle tool with settings.

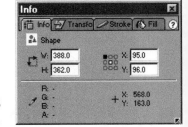

FIGURE 7–26
Info panel.

9. Important: Deselect this rectangle! Change to the Text tool. Open the Character panel and choose Impact or the font of your choice, a font size of 36, and white for the color.

10. Type the phrase "Stitch Comment Form."

11. Deselect this text and change to a font size of 20.

12. Type the words "Subject" and "Body."

13. Deselect this text. Open the Text Options panel, shown in Figure 7–27. Select Input Text from the drop-down box on this panel. When you use the Text tool, you will draw a text input box.

14. Use the Text Tool to draw two input boxes. The font selection and size will be what appears in the box when the form is used in a browser. Make sure you change the color to black in the Character panel so that the text will show up when input.

15. Reposition and resize the items on the page to resemble the screen shot in Figure 7–24. We need only add the Submit button.

16. Flash 5 has some premade form controls. To use their premade button for the form, choose Window➔Common Libraries➔Buttons.

17. Select the button of your choice from the list and drag it onto the work area. The sample page uses Push Bar. You can close the Library now.

18. Edit your button and add the word OK or Submit to the Up, Over, and Down keyframes. You should make sure the Text Options panel is set to Static Text.

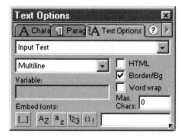

FIGURE 7–27
Text tool settings.

Setting the Variables

The next step is to assign the values of the text boxes to variables. When the form is submitted, these are the values that will be sent to the mail message.

1. Make sure the Text Options panel is open and select the top text input.
2. Type "subject" for the Variable value. Click in the Border/Bg checkbox. See Figure 7–28.
3. Select the second text input box. Type "body" for the Variable value. Click in the Border/Bg checkbox. Also choose Multiline from the second drop-down box.

Creating a New Scene

We need to create another scene that can be displayed when the message is sent.

1. Choose Insert→Scene.
2. You will automatically change to the new scene.
3. Set the Text Options panel back to Static Text. Use the Text tool to type "Thanks for your comments." Make this fairly large and centered.

Adding the Actions

1. Return to the first scene.
2. We need to add a Stop action to this scene so that the movie will not play the second scene automatically. Double-click the keyframe to open the Frame Actions dialog. Double-click on Stop from the Basic Actions menu. Close this dialog.

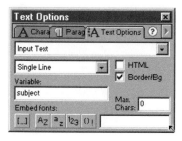

FIGURE 7–28
Text Options panel.

3. Select the button we added to the form.
4. Choose Window→Actions to open the Object Actions dialog.
5. Double-click on On Mouse Event from Basic Actions. Select Press for the Event on the bottom of the dialog.
6. Double-click on Get URL. Okay, this next bit is a little tricky. First, click in the Expression checkbox immediately to the right of the URL blank. On the bottom, for URL, enter this string (include the quotes):

    ```
    "mailto:someone@someaddress.com?subject=
    "+subject+"&body="+body
    ```

    where someone@someaddress.com is the email address you want this form to be sent to. See Figure 7–29.
7. Leave the Window drop-down blank and choose Don't Send for the Variables drop-down.
8. We need to tell the button to change to the other scene when it is pressed. Double-click on Go To from the Basic Actions menu.
9. On the bottom of the dialog, choose Scene 2 for Scene and Frame Number 1. See Figure 7–30. Uncheck Go to and Play.

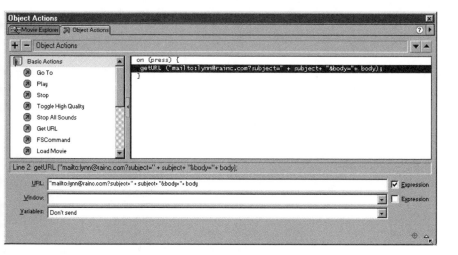

FIGURE 7–29 Actions tab with Get URL action added.

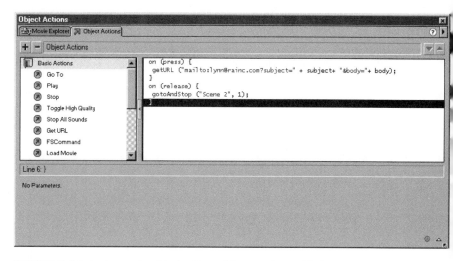

FIGURE 7–30 Actions tab with Go To and Stop action added

That's it! To publish, you need to create an HTML and a Flash file under Formats in the Publish Settings. This is a very simple form that may not work on all browsers. The point here is that variables can be sent using POST or GET to another URL with the Get URL action on the button. The URL can be the location of a script, where the variables can be parsed and used.

CHECKPOINT
This would be a good time to save your work. Choose File→ Save As, and save this file in the directory of your choice as *shelley.fla*. Download the project at this point from
http://www.phptr.com/essential/flash5
or view it directly at
http://www.phptr.com/essential/flash5/stitch/form7-1.html.

We will now move on to the interactive activity planned for this site: a virtual dressing room!

◆ Interactive Activity

Since *Stitch* is a fashion site, it makes sense that the site should promote the sale of clothes. The *Stitch* dressing room is an interactive page that lets the viewer change the color of the clothes being displayed. Figure 7–31 will give you an idea of what the first part of the final movie will look like.

Getting Started

This interactive activity is not part of the other movie. You will need to create a new movie.

1. Choose File→New.
2. Make sure View→Antialias Text is on.

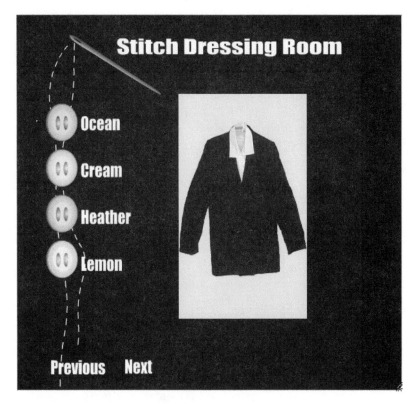

FIGURE 7–31 Stitch Dressing Room.

3. Get out of the work area view mode by unchecking View→Work Area.

4. Choose Modify→Movie, and make the movie size 600 pixels by 500 pixels.

5. Set the background color to the same blue as you used in the other movie. Click OK.

6. Select File→Open as Library and choose the most recent *stitch.fla*. This opens only the Library dialog box associate with the file.

7. Save the new file as *room.fla*.

CHECKPOINT

This would be a good time to save your work. Choose File→Save As, and save this file in the directory of your choice as *shelley.fla*. Download the project at this point from
http://www.phptr.com/essential/flash5
or view it directly at
http://www.phptr.com/essential/flash5/stitch/room7-1.html.

The entire activity consists of two frames, each of which contains four different colored buttons, four photos, a Previous and Next button, and some static graphics. Unlike previous movies you've created, this one does not have any animation. Rather, the photograph changes when one of the buttons is pressed.

Adding the Static Elements

1. Type the words "Stitch Dressing Room" with the Text tool, using the same font you used for the main site, font size of 24, and a white color.

2. Using the same settings, type the word "Previous" and the word "Next." These should be separate text items.

3. Select the Previous label and choose Insert→Convert to Symbol. Name it "Previous" and make it a button.

4. Select the Next label and choose Insert→Convert to Symbol. Name it "Next" and make it a button.

5. Using the Library dialog box for *stitch.fla,* which you opened earlier, find the Needle graphic.

6. Drag the Needle image into the scene.

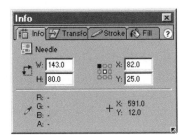

FIGURE 7–32
Info panel.

7. Open the Info panel and change the values for the Needle image to those shown in Figure 7–32. This is a width of 143, a height of 80, an X of 82, and a Y of 25.

8. Change the Stitch Dressing Room text location and size to the values shown in Figure 7–33. Click Apply. This is a width of 360, a height of 37, an X of 152, and a Y of 22.

9. Drag the Thread symbol into the scene. It will need to be resized and rotated by hand to match the screen shot in Figure 7–31.

10. Move the Next and Previous buttons to the approximate locations shown.

11. Insert a keyframe at frame 2.

12. Close the *stitch.fla* Library window.

CHECKPOINT
This would be a good time to save your work. Choose File→Save As, and save this file in the directory of your choice as *shelley.fla*. Download the project at this point from
http://www.phptr.com/essential/flash5
or view it directly at
http://www.phptr.com/essential/flash5/stitch/room7-2.html.

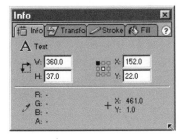

FIGURE 7–33
Info panel.

Creating a Movie Clip

Instead of calling each photo when the appropriate button is pressed, we will call a particular frame in a movie clip.

1. Choose Window→Library to open the Library for the current dialog box.
2. From the Options menu on the Library, choose New Symbol.
3. Name it "Colors" and make it a movie clip. Click OK.
4. You are now in symbol editing mode for the new symbol you just created. Insert three keyframes right next to each other, as shown in Figure 7–34.
5. Download the following files from *http://www.phptr.com/essential/flash5/stitch/misc/room/*:
   ocean.jpg, heather.jpg, cream.jpg, lemon.jpg, denim.jpg, gold.jpg, jade.jpg, and brick.jpg
6. Click on the first keyframe. Choose File→Import and locate *ocean.jpg*.
7. Click on the second keyframe and import *cream.jpg*.
8. Click on the third keyframe and import *heather.jpg*.
9. Click on the fourth one and import *lemon.jpg*.
10. Return to the first keyframe and open the Frame panel.
11. Locate the Label blank and type in "ocean," as shown in Figure 7–35.
12. Repeat this Labeling for the other three images, naming them, in order, "cream," "heather," and "lemon."

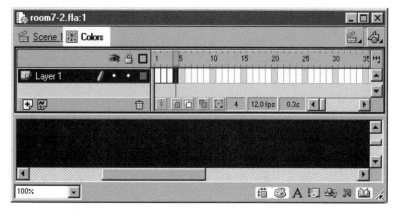

FIGURE 7–34 Three keyframes added to Layer 1.

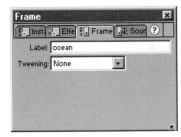

FIGURE 7–35
Frame panel.

CHECKPOINT

This would be a good time to save your work. Choose File→Save As, and save this file in the directory of your choice as *shelley.fla.* Download the project at this point from
http://www.phptr.com/essential/flash5
or view it directly at
http://www.phptr.com/essential/flash5/stitch/room7-3.html.

Adding the Colored Buttons

1. Choose Edit→Edit Movie. Click on the first keyframe.
2. Select File→Open as Library and choose *stitch.fla.*
3. Find the Parent button in the Library.
4. Drag four instances of the Parent button into the scene. See Figure 7–36.
5. Line them up on the thread, as shown earlier in Figure 7–31. Use the Grid and Snap options as well as the Align panel to assist you.
6. Change to the second keyframe and drag four instances into this frame as well. Line them up.
7. Return to the first keyframe and select just the top button.
8. Open the Effect panel.
9. Choose Tint from the drop-down box.
10. Change the Tint Percentage to 40% and the RGB color to 17, 250, 255, as shown in Figure 7–37.
11. Repeat the process for the second button, choosing 40%, 232, 224, and 216.
12. Change the third and fourth buttons also. The third button should be colored 153, 204, 255. The fourth should be 255, 255, 102. Use 40% for both.

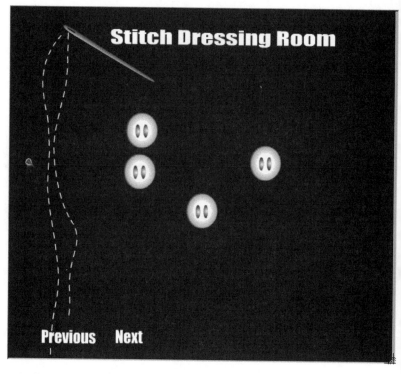

FIGURE 7–36 Four instances of Parent button on scene.

13. Change to the second keyframe. Change the color of the first button to 73, 152, 248 and the Tint to 40%.
14. Change the second, third and fourth buttons also. The second button should be colored 233, 222, 107. The third button should be colored 81, 232, 53. The fourth should be 208, 40, 41. Use 40% for all three.

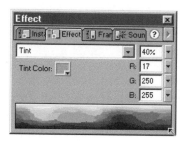

FIGURE 7–37
Color Effect tab for top button.

CHECKPOINT

This would be a good time to save your work. Choose File→Save As, and save this file in the directory of your choice as *shelley.fla*. Download the project at this point from
http://www.phptr.com/essential/flash5
or view it directly at
http://www.phptr.com/essential/flash5/stitch/room7-4.html.

Adding Some Text Labels

1. Select the first keyframe. Use the text tool to add the color labels next to each button, as shown in Figure 7–38.
2. Align the text labels so that they line up with the buttons. Use the Align panel to help.

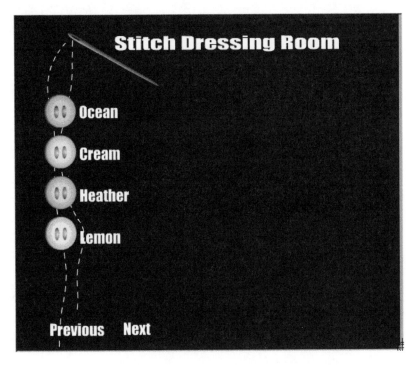

FIGURE 7–38 Color labels added to each button for first keyframe.

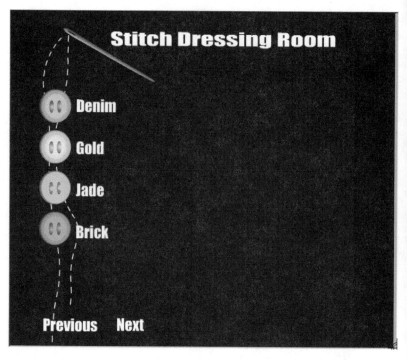

FIGURE 7–39 Color labels added to each button for second keyframe.

3. Select the second keyframe and add the labels shown in Figure 7–39.
4. Move the text labels so that they line up with the buttons.

Applying the Action to the First Button

Each one of the buttons will call a particular frame of the movie you created.

1. First, drag an instance of the Colors movie into the first keyframe of the main movie from the Library dialog box.
2. Open the Instance panel.
3. Set the Name to Suit. Leave the Behavior set to Movie Clip. See Figure 7–40.
4. Select the button with the Ocean label next to it. This is the top button on the first keyframe.
5. Choose Window→Actions.
6. Select On Mouse Event from the Basic Actions menu.

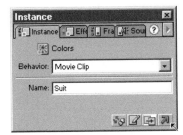

FIGURE 7–40
Instance panel.

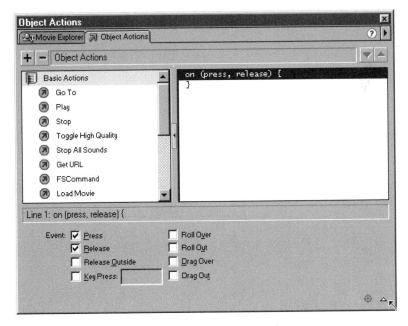

FIGURE 7–41 Actions tab with On Mouse Event action added.

7. On the bottom of the dialog box, click in the Press and Release checkboxes, as shown in Figure 7–41.
8. Now double-click on Tell Target from the Basic Actions menu.
9. On the bottom of the dialog box type "Suit" for Target.
10. Double-click on Go To from the Basic Actions menu.
11. Change Type to Frame Label and type in "ocean" in the blank next to Frame. Uncheck the Go to and Play checkbox. You can leave the Object Actions dialog open.

CHECKPOINT

This would be a good time to save your work. Choose File→Save As, and save this file in the directory of your choice as *shelley.fla*. Download the project at this point from
http://www.phptr.com/essential/flash5
or view it directly at
http://www.phptr.com/essential/flash5/stitch/room7-5.html.

Applying the Action to the Second Button

1. If the Object Actions dialog is not open, open it by choosing Window→Actions.
2. Select the second button in the first keyframe located next to the word Cream.
3. Select On Mouse Event from the Basic Actions menu.
4. On the bottom of the dialog box, click in the Press and Release checkboxes.
5. Now double-click on Tell Target from the Basic Actions menu, as shown in Figure 7–42.
6. On the bottom of the dialog box type "Suit" for Target.
7. Double-click on Go To from the Basic Actions menu.
8. Change Type to Frame Label and type in "cream" in the blank next to Frame. Uncheck the Go to and Play checkbox, as shown in Figure 7–43.

Applying Actions to the Third and Fourth Buttons

Repeat steps 1 through 8 for the third and fourth buttons. The only difference for each button is step 8. The Label for step 8 should be "heather" for the third button and "lemon" for the fourth. You can change to Expert mode by clicking on the small black arrow on the upper right of the dialog and cut and paste the code.

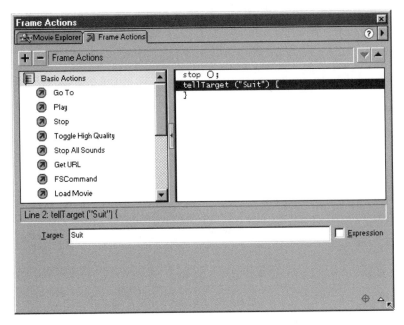

FIGURE 7–42 Actions tab with Go To and Stop action added.

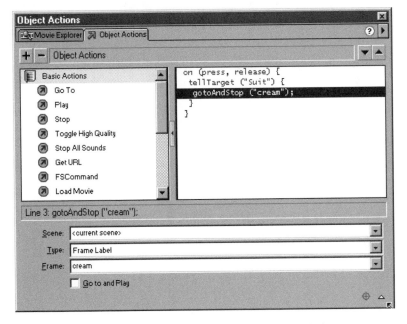

FIGURE 7–43 Actions tab with Go To and Stop action added.

CHECKPOINT

This would be a good time to save your work. Choose File→Save As, and save this file in the directory of your choice as *shelley.fla.* Download the project at this point from
http://www.phptr.com/essential/flash5
or view it directly at
http://www.phptr.com/essential/flash5/stitch/room7-6.html.

Setting Actions for the First Keyframe

If you tried to play the movie right now, all it would do is keep playing swapping between the two frames. We need to apply some actions to the keyframes.

1. Select the first keyframe.
2. Open the Frame panel and enter the name "Suit."
3. Choose Window→Actions to open the Frame Actions dialog.
4. Double-click on Stop from the Basic Actions menu.
5. Next, double-click on Tell Target.
6. Type in "Suit" for the Target.
7. Now double-click on Go To and select Frame Number for Type.
8. Put the number 1 in the Frame blank. See Figure 7–44. Uncheck the Go to and Play box.

Creating the Movie Clip for the Second Keyframe

To put together the second keyframe, you will need another movie clip.

1. Choose Window→Library to open the Library.
2. From the Options menu on this dialog box, choose New Symbol.
3. Name it "Colors2" and make it a movie clip. Click OK.
4. Insert three more keyframes right next to each other.
5. Click on the first keyframe. Choose File→Import and choose *denim.jpg.*

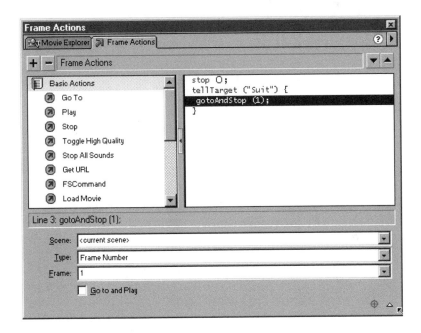

FIGURE 7–44 Actions tab with Go To and Stop action added.

6. Click on the second keyframe and import *gold.jpg*.
7. Click on the third keyframe and import *jade.jpg*.
8. Click on the fourth one and import *brick.jpg*.
9. Return to the first keyframe and open the Frame panel.
10. Type "denim" for Label.
11. Repeat for the other three images, naming them, in order, "gold," "jade," and "brick."

CHECKPOINT
This would be a good time to save your work. Choose File→Save As, and save this file in the directory of your choice as *shelley.fla*. Download the project at this point from
http://www.phptr.com/essential/flash5
or view it directly at
http://www.phptr.com/essential/flash5/stitch/room7-7.html.

Applying the Action to the First Button

1. Choose Edit→Edit Movie. Select keyframe 2.
2. Drag an instance of the Colors2 movie from the Library dialog box onto keyframe 2 of the scene.
3. Select this instance.
4. Open the Instance panel.
5. Set the Name to Shirt, as shown in Figure 7–45. Leave the Behavior set to Movie Clip.
6. Select the blue button with the text label Denim next to it.
7. Choose Window→Actions.
8. Select On Mouse Event from the Basic Actions menu.
9. On the bottom of the dialog box, click in the Press and Release checkboxes, as shown in Figure 7–46.
10. Now double-click on Tell Target from the Basic Actions menu.
11. On the bottom of the dialog box type "Shirt" for Target.
12. Double-click on Go To from the Basic Actions menu.
13. Change Type to Frame Label and type in "denim" in the blank next to Frame. Uncheck the Go to and Play checkbox, as shown in Figure 7–47.

In order to apply actions to the second, third, and fourth buttons, repeat steps 7 through 13 for the second, third, and fourth buttons. The Label for step 8 should be "gold" for the second button, "jade" for the third button, and "brick" for the fourth.

CHECKPOINT

This would be a good time to save your work. Choose File→Save As, and save this file in the directory of your choice as *shelley.fla*. Download the project at this point from
http://www.phptr.com/essential/flash5
or view it directly at
http://www.phptr.com/essential/flash5/stitch/room7-8.html.

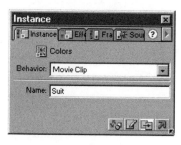

FIGURE 7–45
Instance panel.

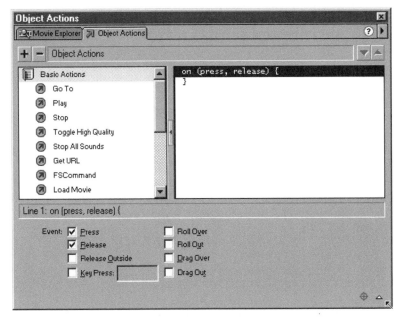

FIGURE 7–46 Actions tab with On Mouse Event action added.

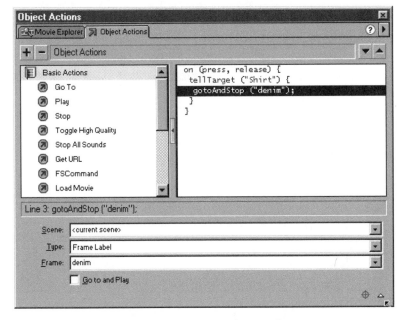

FIGURE 7–47 Actions tab with Go To and Stop action added.

Setting Actions for the Second Keyframe

1. Select the second keyframe.
2. Open the Frame panel and enter the name "Shirt."
3. Choose Window→Actions to open the Frame Actions dialog.
4. Double-click on Stop from the Basic Actions menu.
5. Next, double-click on Tell Target.
6. Type in "Shirt" for the Target.
7. Now double-click on Go To and select Frame Number for Type.
8. Put the number 2 in the Frame blank. See Figure 7–48. Uncheck the Go to and Play box.

Adding Next and Previous Buttons

The final thing for the activity to work is the addition of the Next and Previous actions. Since you only have two frames, the Next and Previous buttons will both point to the same thing on the frame. On keyframe 1, they will both call the second frame,

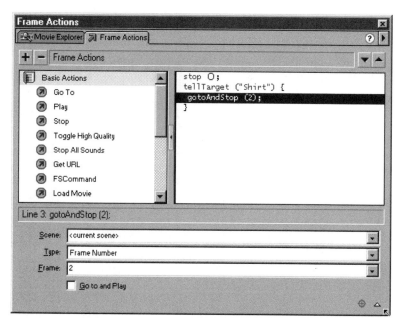

FIGURE 7–48 Actions tab with Go To and Stop action added.

which you named "Shirt." On keyframe 2, they will both call the first frame, which you called "Suit." Obviously, if you had more frames, you would have to change where they pointed.

1. Click on the first keyframe.
2. Deselect everything and then use the Arrow to select the Next button.
3. Choose Window→Actions
4. Double-click on On Mouse Event from the Basic Actions menu.
5. On the bottom, select the Release checkbox, shown in Figure 7–49.
6. Double-click on Go To from the Basic Actions menu. Uncheck Go to and Play.
7. On the bottom, select Frame Label for Type and enter "Shirt" in the Frame blank.
8. Select the Previous button and follow steps 3 through 7.
9. Change to the second keyframe.
10. Use the Arrow to select just the Next button.
11. Choose Window→Actions.

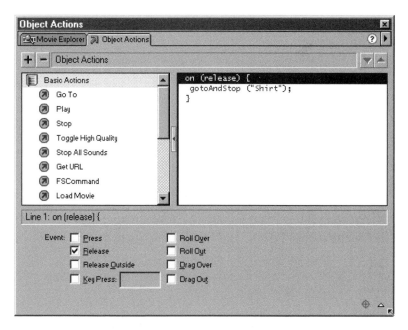

FIGURE 7–49 Actions tab with On Mouse Event action added.

12. Double-click on On Mouse Event from the Basic Actions menu.
13. On the bottom, select the Release checkbox.
14. Double-click on Go To from the Basic Actions menu. Uncheck Go to and Play.
15. On the bottom, select Frame Label for Type and enter "Suit" in the Frame blank.
16. Select the Previous button and follow steps 11 through 15.

CHECKPOINT

This would be a good time to save your work. Choose File→ Save As, and save this file in the directory of your choice as *shelley.fla.* Download the project at this point from
http://www.phptr.com/essential/flash5
or view it directly at
http://www.phptr.com/essential/flash5/stitch/room7-9.html.

You have finished! To test the activity, choose Control→ Test Movie.

Uh-oh...we forgot one thing—a link to this movie from the main site!

1. Open *stitch.fla.*
2. Choose the Menu scene from the Scene List button on the top right.
3. Select the Links layer and choose its last keyframe. Deselect everything.
4. Use the Text tool to type "Visit the Stitch Dressing Room," as shown in Figure 7–31. The font is Impact, font size is 24, and color is white.
5. Select the text with the Arrow tool and choose Insert→ Convert to Symbol.
6. Name it "Visit" and make it a button.
7. Select it and choose Edit→ Edit Symbols.
8. Insert a keyframe on Over.
9. Select the text, change to the Text tool, and change the color to light blue.

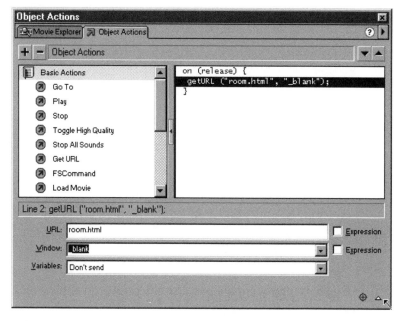

FIGURE 7–50 Actions tab with Get URL action added.

10. Choose Edit→Edit Movie and select the Visit button.
11. Choose Window'Actions. Double-click on Get URL from the Basic Actions menu. Enter *room.html* for the URL on the bottom and choose *_blank* for the Window. See Figure 7–50. Close this dialog.

If you were using frames, you could control which frame is loaded on button clicks by using this technique and changing the Window setting.

CHECKPOINT
Download the project at this point from
http://www.phptr.com/essential/flash5
or view it directly at
http://www.phptr.com/essential/flash5/stitch/stitch7-8.html.

Final Production: Publishing

You called *room.html* in the button action above, but that file does not yet exist. For that matter, the *stitch.fla* file has not yet been made into a movie. Let's fix that.

1. Open both *room.fla* and *stitch.fla.*
2. Choose File➔Publish Settings for each. Both will need an HTML and a Flash file created under the Formats tab. For the most part, the default values should be used. You may want to play with the JPEG compression setting to achieve a middle ground between reasonable file size and reasonable image quality.

Test your movies in your Web browser and play with the Publish settings. You may prefer to set the movie size to match the browser rather than the movie file. These files may take a little while to download over a network.

You have now learned all the essentials of Flash 5 creation and production. Flash is an extremely powerful Web tool, and its use is limited only by your imagination.

RECAP

In this chapter you've learned how to:
- Create animated buttons
- Make a transition from one scene to another
- Open movies in other browser windows
- Create a comment form
- Create an interactive movie

A Glossary

ACTIONS

Actions are behaviors that can be assigned to frames or buttons. These can be triggered by specific events occurring in the movie or from user interaction with the movie. To access the Actions interface, select the frame or button you want to add actions to and choose Window→ Actions. Click on the button with the plus sign. Only Basic Actions are mentioned below. With Flash 5, Macromedia has provided excellent documentation of all the advanced options.

Go To is used to make the movie go to another frame, scene, or movie. It can be set to either **Go To and Play** or **Go To and Stop** to control the behavior of the movie.

Toggle High Quality turns antialiasing on or off. If there is a section of your movie that you do not need to deliver in high quality, turning this off allows faster download at the expense of image quality.

Stop All Sounds stops any sounds being played by the movie.

Get URL is used to make buttons or frames fetch a particular URL. It also allows you to specify a window or html frame in which the new URL will appear.

The **FS Command** action is used to communicate with the program hosting the Flash player, such as a browser or standalone projector.

Load/Unload Movie loads or unloads a movie located at the specified URL. Loaded movies can be given level numbers or expressions with this action type to allow identification and ordering.

Tell Target creates a program block used for sending commands to an instance of a symbol or movie. The instance must be given a label name, and the Tell Target must be given this name. Every action in the Tell Target block will then be applied to the target. Tell Target was used in the Stitch Dressing Room movie to specify which image in the target movie to display when the corresponding button was pressed.

If Frame is Loaded creates an IF program block used for executing commands if the named frame has been loaded. This is especially useful for preloading.

On Mouse Event is an action used by button instances. When the specified mouse action or actions take place, the commands are carried out. Selecting this action and choosing the Key Press option will detect keyboard events.

If creates an expression to be evaluated and a program block that is executed if the condition is met.

Loop creates an expression to be evaluated and a program block that is executed until the condition is no longer met.

Call can be used to call a frame and execute its actions.

Set Property allows you to change one of the properties of a target. Properties include the X and Y locations, visibility, and height and width, among many others.

Set Variable allows you to set or change the value of a variable.

Duplicate/Remove Movie Clip allows you to duplicate or remove clips. Duplicate allows you to specify the target, give the movie a new name, and give it a depth value.

Drag Movie Clip causes the movie clip instance specified by the target movie to follow the mouse cursor as it is moved. In Flash 5, you can hide the mouse cursor at the same time, so the dragged movie clip appears to be the cursor when it is over the movie.

Trace is used to track the value of variables, specifically for debugging. A window opens and displays the specified values.

Comment is used to add a comment at any point to the Action code you have created.

FIGURE A-1
The Align panel.

ALIGN PANEL

The Align panel is used to align or match the sizes of more than one object. The Align panel can also be used to evenly distribute the space between groups of objects. See Figure A-1.

ANTIALIAS

Antialias is a display mode that smoothes the edges of lines and shapes. It can be toggled on or off using the menu option View➔ Antialias.

ANTIALIAS TEXT

Antialias Text is a display mode that smoothes the edges of text created in Flash. It can be toggled on or off using the menu option View➔ Antialias Text.

ARRANGE

The menu option Modify➔ Arrange is used to access several ordering commands. These commands are used to change the order of graphic objects and text within a single layer.

ARROW

The Arrow tool is used to select, move, scale, and rotate graphics. It can also be used to add and modify curves on lines and shapes. To select multiple objects, use the Arrow and the Shift key. When an object is selected, clicking on it and dragging will move it. When the Scale or Rotate button is on, the currently selected object can be scaled or rotated by using the handles. The Smooth and Straighten buttons can be used to smooth or straighten curved lines. Finally, when the Arrow is placed on an unselected line or the edge of a shape and the cursor changes, clicking and dragging will curve the object.

BREAK APART

Modify→Break Apart ungroups grouped objects, text objects, symbols, and bitmaps. This makes it possible to edit parts of these objects.

BRUSH

The Brush tool is used to create free-form images. The Brush controls include:

Brush Mode, which controls what can be painted. Paint Normal applies the brush anywhere. Paint Fills applies the brush only to other fills, leaving lines alone. Paint Behind paints only on empty areas. Paint Selection applies the brush to selected fills only. Paint Inside paints only over the inside fill at the place where you begin painting.

Fill Color controls the color that the brush paints. This may also be a gradient fill.

Brush Size is used to set the size of the brush stroke.

Brush Shape is used to set the shape of the brush stroke.

CHARACTER PANEL

Use the Character panel to set the font, font size, font color, and font style.

CONTROLLING MOVIES

The Menu option Control contains several commands for testing the movie being created.

Play plays the current movie in the scene from the current frame to the end.

Rewind returns to the first keyframe.

Step Forward sets the current frame to the next in sequence.

Step Backward sets the current frame to the previous in sequence.

Test Movie plays the current movie and all its scenes in a separate window. The movie loops until the window is closed.

Debug Movie opens the Debugger panel. This panel allows you to watch the values of variables and modify their values as the movie plays.

Test Scene plays only the current scene in a separate window. The scene loops until the window is closed.

Loop Playback is an option. When selected, the Play command loops repeatedly.

Play All Scenes is an option. When selected, the Play command plays through all scenes of the current movie.

Enable Simple Frame Actions is an option. When selected, the Play command executes any frame actions in the movie.

Enable Simple Buttons is an option. When selected, buttons are active and will display their states in response to the mouse actions. The buttons will be active whether or not the movie is playing.

Enable Sounds is an option. When selected, the Play command will execute any sounds embedded in the movie.

CONVERT LINES TO FILLS

Convert Lines to Fills, located under the Modify→Shape menu, converts any selected line into an identical fill.

DRAWING

Curves can be drawn with the Pencil tool set in either Smooth or Ink Pencil Mode. Curves can also be added to existing lines using the Arrow tool, or created with Bezier curves using the Pen tool.

Lines can be drawn with the Line tool.

Ovals can be drawn with the Oval tool.

Rectangles can be drawn with the Rectangle tool.

DROPPER

The Dropper tool is used to determine the fill or line style of any graphic. When clicked on a fill, the settings used for that fill are selected by default for the Paint Bucket and Brush tools. When used on a line, the settings for that line are selected by default for the Pencil and Line tools.

EFFECT PANEL

Change the color tinting or transparency of a symbol instance with this panel.

ERASER

The Eraser tool is used to erase portions of images. The Eraser controls include:

Eraser Mode controls what can be painted on. Erase Normal applies the eraser anywhere. Erase Fills erases fills only, leaving lines alone. Erase Line erases lines only, leaving fills alone. Erase Selected Fills applies the eraser to selected fills only. Erase Inside erases only the inside fill where you begin painting.

The **Faucet** option deletes an entire fill area or line segment.

Eraser Shape is used to set the size and shape of the eraser.

EXPAND FILL

Expand Fill, located under the Modify→ Shape menu, expands or contracts a fill a specified number of pixels.

FILL PANEL

The Fill panel is used to create and modify fill types between Linear Gradient, Radial Gradient, and Solid.

FILLS

Gradient fills are area fills consisting of more than one color. They can be created by accessing the Fill panel. Click on the Gradient tab. The two types of gradient fills are linear and radial. Both types can contain from two to eight colors. Individual colors can also be set to transparent using the Alpha slider on the Mixer panel. See Figure A–2.

Solid fills are area fills consisting of colors of varying transparency. Accessing the Mixer panel from the palette of any of the

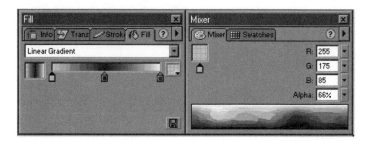

FIGURE A–2 The Gradient panel and Mixer panel.

line, shape, or fill tools can change the fill color. Colors can be set to levels of transparency using the Alpha slider.

FRAME PANEL

Use the Frame panel to set tweening type, tweening options, and label names for frames.

FRAMES

Frames are still images, displayed for discrete moments in time for each layer. Animation in Flash consists of each frame being shown in order. The speed at which the frames are displayed is controlled by the fps (frames per second) setting in Flash. A setting of 12 fps, which is the default setting, means that 12 frames will be displayed every second. The fps setting can be changed using the Movie Properties dialog.

GRID

The grid consists of horizontal and vertical lines, useful for placing graphic elements during development. The distance between the grid lines can be changed using View→ Grid→ Edit Grid. The View→ Grid→ Snap to Grid option causes graphic elements to align themselves along grid lines automatically when they are created, modified, or moved.

GROUP

Several graphic objects can be combined together using the Group command. To use it, select more than one object and choose Modify→ Group. When objects are grouped, they can be moved, resized, and rotated at the same time. They maintain their integrity, and can be Ungrouped.

HAND

The Hand tool moves the viewing area. It has no effect on graphic elements.

INFO PANEL

The Info panel can be used to see and modify the height, width, x location, and y location of graphics.

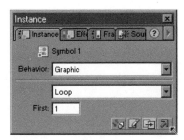

FIGURE A–3
The Instance Properties panel.

INSTANCE PROPERTIES

Instance properties are used to modify symbols at specific key-frames. The Instance panel can be accessed by selecting a specific symbol at a keyframe and choosing Modify→Instance. The Instance tab specifies a label name for the instance as well as its behavior at that keyframe. See Figure A–3. The Effect tab can be used to change the color or transparency of the symbol at that keyframe.

IMPORT

The menu option File→Import places a graphic or sound file in the current movie's library. It can then be added to the movie.

INK BOTTLE

To change an existing line's color, size, and style, use the Ink Bottle tool. To change multiple different lines at once, select them all and use the Ink Bottle. The settings on the Ink Bottle are Line Color, Line Size, and Line Style.

INSTANCE PANEL

The Instance panel is used to modify a specific instance of a symbol. You can change the symbol type here of a symbol instance without changing the parent symbol type. This is also where you give instance names to movie clips.

KEYFRAMES

Keyframes are special types of frames where actions or animation changes can be set. They serve as placeholders on the Timeline where any symbol's animated behavior changes, starts, or stops. Frames, which are static, mark continuing motion between keyframes. Changes or actions cannot be set in a frame that is not a keyframe. When you create frame-by-frame animation, every frame is a keyframe. In tweened animation, you define keyframes at important points in the animation and let Flash control the content of frames between those points. Keyframes exist in specific layers and can be created by selecting a layer and a specific frame and choosing Insert Keyframe.

LASSO

The Lasso tool is used to select portions of a graphic element rather than the entire thing. The Magic Wand modifier can be used to select colors in a particular area. The color at the first point that you click with the Magic Wand, as well as all other colors that fall within the specified tolerance, are ignored. All other colors in the Lasso area are selected. You can modify the color tolerance with the Magic Wand Properties button. The Polygon option makes the Lasso draw straight lines.

LAYERS

Layers are used to separate graphic objects and symbols, to allow more control. The currently selected layer has a black label with white text and a pencil icon to the right of its name. Only one symbol in a layer may be animated, so multiple animated symbols require multiple layers. Each layer can contain keyframes at different locations. To create a layer, choose the menu option Insert Layer. To rename a layer, double-click on its name. There is also a special type of layer called a Motion Guide, used for creating animation paths for symbols to follow. See Figure A–4.

LAYER VIEWS

When you deal with more than one layer, it is possible to hide, lock, and view outlines of the other layers. Hiding the other layers leaves only one layer's contents visible on the scene. Locking the other layers leaves all the other contents visible, but not editable.

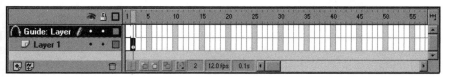

FIGURE A–4 Layers.

Viewing outlines converts all the graphics in a particular layer to outlines of a single color. To hide or lock layers, click under the eye icon or the lock icon. The outlines can be turned on by clicking under the small square next to the lock icon. Also, the Layer menu can be used. The Layer menu is accessible by right-clicking (PC) or Ctrl-clicking (Mac) on a layer.

LIBRARIES

The Libraries menu item contains already created buttons, sounds, symbols, components, and movie clips from Macromedia.

LIBRARY

The Library panel contains all the symbols in a movie. Instances of symbols can be dragged from this panel onto the current scene. The Library contains graphic symbols, sounds, and imported images. See Figure A–5.

LINE TOOL

The Line tool is used to draw straight lines. The settings for lines can be set in the Stroke panel. These are Line Color, Line Size, and Line Style.

MAGNIFIER

The Magnifier tool is used to zoom the view of the scene in and out. This is also controlled by the Zoom drop-down box on the bottom left of the stage. The two modifiers are Enlarge and

FIGURE A–5
The Library panel.

Reduce. When the view is reduced, the zoomed-in scene is centered at the spot on the scene where the Magnifier was clicked.

MIXER PANEL

The Mixer panel is used to select colors. You can set them by RGB and also adjust their Alpha, or transparency, with this panel.

MOVIE PROPERTIES

The Movie Properties panel can be opened by choosing Modify→ Movie. See Figure A–6.

Frame Rate controls how many frames per second are played when the movie is viewed.

Dimensions are the width and height of the movie in pixels. The units can be changed using the Ruler Units drop-down menu at the bottom of this panel.

The **Match Printer** and **Contents** buttons set the movie dimensions based on the printer settings or the contents of the movie.

MOVIES

Movies in Flash consist of all the keyframes, actions, sounds, layers, and scenes located together in the same .fla file.

ONION SKINS

The Onion Skins setting displays multiple frames of an animation at the same time. The Onion Skin button is directly beneath the Timeline under all the layers. The Onion Skin Outline button displays the multiple frames as outlines. When either of the two buttons is selected, the Onion Skin Markers appear on the Time-

FIGURE A–6 The Movie Properties panel.

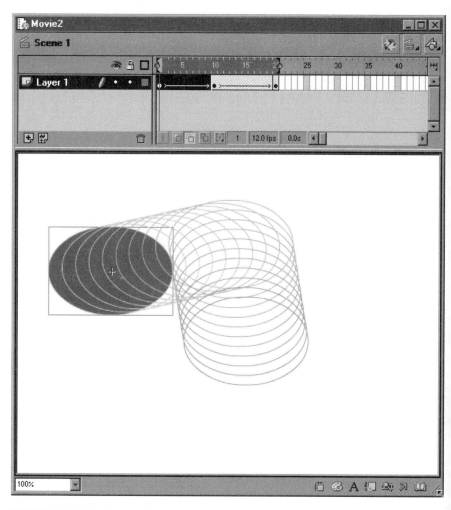

FIGURE A–7 The Onion Skin outlines.

line and can be moved to set the beginning and ending of the displayed sequence. See Figure A–7.

OUTLINES

The View Outlines command displays all the graphics on the scene as outlines.

OVAL TOOL

The Oval tool is used to draw circles and oval shapes. The settings for the oval include:

Line Color, which can be set as any solid color with partial or full transparency

Line Thickness

Line Style

Fill Color, which can be any solid or gradient fill with partial or full transparency

PAINT BUCKET

The Paint Bucket is used to add or replace a current fill to a graphic object. The Gap Size drop-down box specifies what size gaps in an object's border are permissible for it to still be filled. The Paint Bucket can also be used to modify existing gradient fills using the Transform Fill option. The Lock Fill option allows you to extend the same gradient fill across multiple filled objects.

PARAGRAPH PANEL

Set paragraph alignment and margins with this panel.

PUBLISH

The menu option File→Publish uses the current Publish Settings and generates the appropriate files.

PUBLISH PREVIEW

File→Publish Preview creates a temporary version of the current movie and opens a browser window to display it.

PUBLISH SETTINGS

File→Publish Settings opens the Publish Settings panel. This panel is used to specify all the files and settings that should be created. The Formats tab displays a number of checkboxes and file types that can be produced, as well as text boxes where they can be given specific names. See Figure A–8.

Flash tab. The Flash tab controls Flash settings. Load Order is the order in which the layers of the movie are loaded. Generate size report produces a text file with information on all the pieces of the final Flash movie and their sizes. This is useful for figuring out

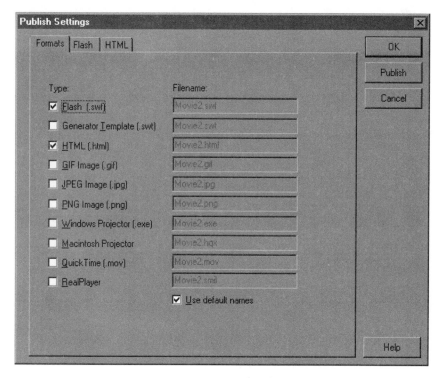

FIGURE A–8 The Publish Settings dialog.

how to optimize the movie. Protect from import keeps the movie file from being downloadable by viewers. The JPEG Quality slider controls the amount of compression Flash uses on any imported images. Audio Stream and Audio Event Set buttons are used to change the streaming and event compressions used. Finally, the Version drop-down is used to specify which version of Flash to create. If Flash 4 is used, any Flash 5 features in the movie will not function. See Figure A–9.

HTML tab. The HTML tab controls how Flash creates HTML files. The Template drop-down contains a variety of precreated HTML templates into which Flash can embed the movie. The Dimensions setting specifies the size at which the movie will be displayed. Setting this to Percent will cause the movie to scale to fit the browser. The other options control how the movie will display, where on the page it will reside, and what menu options will be

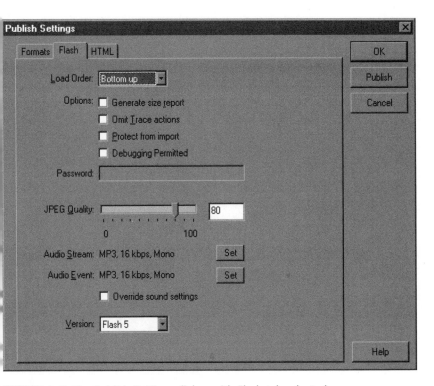

FIGURE A–9 The Publish Settings dialog with Flash tab selected.

available to the viewer who right-clicks or Ctrl-clicks on the movie See Figure A–10.

RECTANGLE TOOL

The Rectangle tool is used to draw squares and rectangle shapes. The settings for the rectangle include:

Line Color, which can be set as any solid color with partial or full transparency

Line Thickness

Line Style

Fill Color, which can be any solid or gradient fill with partial or full transparency

Round Rectangle Radius, which is used to give the rectangle rounded corners

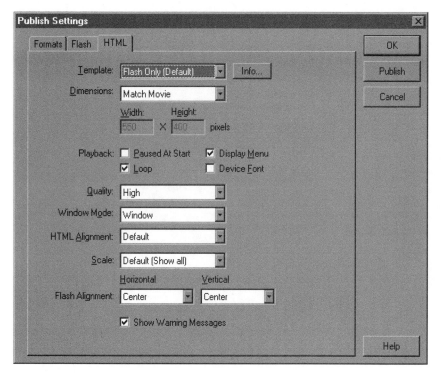

FIGURE A–10 The Publish Settings dialog with HTML tab selected.

ROTATE

The Arrow tool and the Rotate modifier can be used on any selected object. When the Rotate option is on, the selected object displays small handles that can be clicked and dragged to rotate the object. See Figure A–11.

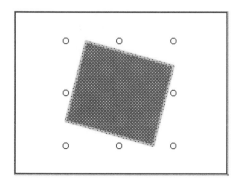

FIGURE A–11
Rotate handles.

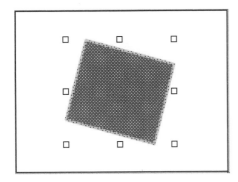

FIGURE A–12
Scale handles.

SCALE

The Arrow tool and the Scale modifier can be used on any selected object. When the Scale option is on, the selected object displays small handles that can be clicked and dragged to scale the object. See Figure A–12.

SCENE PANEL

Use the Scene panel to add, delete, copy, re-order, and rename scenes.

SCENES

Scenes in Flash consist of keyframes, actions, sounds, and layers. A movie may contain multiple scenes.

SELECTING

Graphic objects must be selected to be modified or moved. The Arrow tool is used to select objects. Selected objects are indicated by a crosshatch or checkerboard pattern. Multiple objects can be selected by using the Arrow and clicking and dragging a selection box around them or by using the Arrow and the Shift key.

SHAPE HINTS

Shape hints are used to help control shape tweening. To add shape hints, you must first have created a shape-tweened animation. Clicking on the shape at the first keyframe allows the selection of Modify→Transform→Add Shape Hints. A small circle with a letter appears at either end of the animation. The beginning area this circle is placed on will match the final location of the letter at the last keyframe. See Figure A–13.

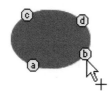

FIGURE A–13
Shape hints.

SMOOTH

To increase the smoothness of a line, the menu option Modify→Smooth can be used. The Arrow tool has a Smooth button that does the same thing.

SNAP TO OBJECTS

Located under the View menu, Snap to Objects can be used to align objects on the scene as they are being created. For example, this can be used to make certain you are creating closed shapes.

SOFTEN FILL EDGES

Soften Fill Edges, located under the Modify→Shape menu, softens the appearance of the edge of a fill a specified number of pixels.

SOUND PANEL

Select and modify sound settings on imported sounds with this panel.

SOUNDS

Flash 5 supports WAV and mp3 sound file types. To use a sound file, it must first be imported using the File Import command. Once imported, it can be dragged from the Library window to keyframes in the main movie or keyframes of buttons.

STRAIGHTEN

To increase the straightness of a line, the menu option Modify→Straighten can be used. The Arrow tool also has a Straighten button that does the same thing.

STROKE PANEL

The Stroke panel is used to specify the style, size, and color of lines.

SWATCHES PANEL

The Swatches panel contains a listing of saved gradients and solid colors.

SYMBOLS

Flash symbols are graphic objects that are stored by Flash. They are important because they can be reused. When you create a symbol, you can use it over and over again without having to redraw it each time you need it, and if you decide to change it, you don't need to change each instance (copy) of it—you can simply change the stored master symbol. Changing the master symbol changes all the instances of it in your Flash movie. There are three types of symbols: graphics, buttons, and movie clips. Graphics are images that can have animation and sounds attached. They are noninteractive. Buttons are graphics that can also respond to mouse actions. Movie clips are entire Flash movies that can be reused inside another movie.

SYMBOLS, CREATING

There are two ways to create a symbol. After you have created a graphic you want to convert, you can either choose the menu option Insert→ Create Symbol or press the F8 key. Once you have created the symbol, it is automatically stored in the local Library.

SYMBOLS, EDITING

There are several ways to edit symbols. In the Library, you can select the symbol you wish to edit and pull up the symbol menu by clicking on the Options button on the top right. You can also choose Edit→ Edit Symbols. Once you are in symbol editing mode, you can switch between symbols by using the Symbol List button on the top right side of the window. See Figure A–14.

FIGURE A–14
The Symbol List button.

TEXT OPTIONS PANEL

The Text Options panel allows you to specify which type of text you want to create. Flash 5 offers you the choice of Input text, such as a text box on a form, Static text, such a label on a page that does not change, and Dynamic text that can be programmatically changed while the movie is running.

TEXT TOOL

The Text tool is used to draw text objects. The settings for text include:

- Font
- Font Size
- Font Color
- Bold and Italic styles
- Alignment
- Paragraph Properties
- Text Input modifier. With this set, the Text tool creates input boxes.

TIMELINE

The Timeline is at the top of the Flash movie editor. The purpose of the Timeline is to serve as a placeholder for the frames in the animation. Using the Timeline menu immediately to the right can modify the view of the Timeline. The Preview and Preview in Context options display thumbnail versions of the graphic objects instead of frames.

TWEENING

Tweening is the process Flash uses to create animation between keyframes by interpolating the intermediate frames. Flash provides a time-saving method of animation that requires only the creation of the most important frames. In using tweening, keyframes serve as turning points during an animation, and Flash fills in the gaps.

TRANSFORM PANEL

The Transform panel can be used to modify the height, width, rotation, and skew of graphics.

TWEENING, MOTION

Motion tweening consists of giving an object a starting and an ending location and letting Flash interpolate the frames between them. Motion tweening also interpolates based on object size and rotation.

TWEENING, SHAPE

Shape tweening animation is used when you need to change or morph one shape into another. The shape and the color shift gradually from the beginning graphic to the final one. As in motion tweening, Flash will interpolate the intermediate frames.

UNGROUP

Modify→Ungroup is used to return objects grouped together using the Group command to their original distinct states.

ZOOM

The Zoom drop-down box is used to zoom the view of the scene in and out. The values in the drop-down box can be selected, and percentages can also be typed into the box. Zoom is also controlled by the Magnifier tool.

Index